MW00478916

Dedicated with Love

to

Joe

who has always supported and encouraged me

TABLE OF CONTENTS

FOREWORD *Bob Russell* ix

INTRODUCTION *Carol Bonura* 1

KIDNAPPED BY CANCER…RANSOMED BY GLORY *Brad Gaines*..7

PERSEVERANCE DEEP WITHIN ME *Joyce Oglesby* 13

DESIRE OF OUR HEARTS *Pat Day* 17

NOT DONE YET *Stephen Tweed*...21

MY AWESOME GOD *Cassie Soete*..29

GOD TO THE RESCUE *Joe Bonura, III* 33

THAT BABY BOY *Lisa Roederer*...39

RATHER HAVE JESUS *Mike Graham*...41

A PERSONAL GOD *Dave Stone* 45

LORD, I WANT TO BE INVISIBLE *Liz Curtis Higgs*...........................47

GOD'S WORD IS POWER *Bob Russell*...51

THE GOD I WORSHIP! *Naomi Rhode*..55

TRUST ME *Willie Jolley* 59

ART OF THE POSSIBLE *Dr. Nido Qubein*...65

HELP MY UNBELIEF *Phillip Van Hooser* 69

LONGING IN MY HEART *Glenna Salsbury* 73

OUR GOD IS A BIG GOD

A PERSONAL MESS *Elizabeth Jeffries* 75

COME TO THE TABLE *Ty Yokum* 79

JUST IN TIME *Katherine Magnuson*..81

THE EPIPHANY *Vince DeSalvo*...85

GIVING THANKS IN ALL CIRCUMSTANCES *Don Waddell* 89

ON THE FRONT END *Gail Wenos* 95

PROTECTED FOR A PURPOSE *Brad DeVries*....................................101

ONE SWIPE OF HIS FINGER *Amos Martin* 105

GOD IN THE MIST *Louise "Nena" Yokum* 107

BLESSED ARE THE MEEK *Margaret Walker* 111

WHEN GOD FINDS YOU IN THE OPRYLAND HOTEL…
Elizabeth Hoagland 117

HEALER, SAVIOR, AND FRIEND *Phyllis Null* 123

SENTENCED TO SERVE *Norb Hancock* 129

DIVINE ORCHESTRATION *Doris Foster* 133

GOD IS ABLE *Aletha Marcum* 137

BRING IT TO ME *Gary Montgomery*..141

WHEN GOD SNEAKS UP ON YOU *Joe Donaldson* 147

WHEN PUSH COMES TO LOVE *Mary Jane Mapes*...........................151

ABIDING LOVE *Mary Rivard*..157

OVERWHELMED! *Greg Allen*...161

GIFTS TO SERVE HIM *Bob Gibson* 163

WHY ME? *Joe Bonura, IV* 167

GOD PREPARED ME *Annie Yoho* 173

IN A HEARTBEAT *Nick Bonura* 177

ALWAYS FAITHFUL *Dorothy Mae Yokum* 181

FINAL NOTE 185

ABOUT THE AUTHOR 187

FOREWORD

Bob Russell, *Retired Senior Pastor of Southeast Christian Church, Louisville, KY*

"Great is our Lord and mighty in power; his understanding has no limit."

(Psalm 147:5)

For the past ten years it has been my privilege to speak in over two hundred churches across America. Almost everywhere I go people ask the same question: "Is there any hope? Do you see any hope for the church and for our country?"

This is an age of despair. Much of the news is dominated by negative stories, stories of scandalized celebrities, broken families, untrustworthy elected officials, and angry underprivileged people. As I write this in the summer of 2016, America is immersed in the most negative, depressing presidential campaign I can recall.

We tune in to the evening news or pick up the morning paper and long for some encouraging stories of hope. Social media, constant exposure to cable news, email, text messages, and the like drown out more important but less dramatic, positive stories.

For these reasons, I think we need some inspiring stories today more than ever. We need to be reminded that we serve an awesome God and nothing is impossible with Him. That's why I am so appreciative that Carol Bonura has compiled this book at this time. In it she highlights 41 stories written by ordinary people, for the most part, like you and me. Here are forty-one stories of hope and blessings from Heaven. She relates examples of ordinary people who have been blessed by an awesome God who wrote the story of creation and followed it up with "the greatest story ever told," the Gospel story of Jesus Christ.

And of course that is the ultimate positive story, the good news, the Gospel which not only inspires but saves and gives us a living, breathing, truly larger-than-life example of how the love of God was extended from Heaven to transform us and give us hope.

In this book you'll find many personal stories in a concerted effort to see God in good times and bad, to see God rise to the occasion and help people be more than they can be alone. I know almost all of the writers who contributed to this book, and I can vouch for their faithfulness and walk with Christ and the Godly example they are to me and others.

Some of their stories are deeply personal, some are dramatic, but all are convicting. Overall, however, is the realization that when we allow the Spirit of God to work through us, we have a positive story to tell to the nations, a story that can change lives and inspire others to be more than they can be alone.

Carol and Joe Bonura are special people who have blessed me and many others at Southeast Christian Church, where we attend. Now Carol has compiled this book to describe by means of storytelling how great our God is. It will bless you by revealing new insights into God's character. It will inspire you to see how God can turn despair into hope. It will help you appreciate that our God is, indeed, an awesome God, an omnipotent God who loves to work through His children in a way that is often best told through the use of stories.

What story is God telling by your life?

INTRODUCTION - CAROL BONURA

R ecently, I vacationed with very dear friends, and we had time in the mornings for serious study of the Book of Ecclesiastes, and we were each to present something on Ecclesiastes.

Have you ever read a Bible verse that opened your mind to consider all the possibilities of the immensity of God? I have that experience every time that I read, "He has made everything beautiful in its time, and He has also set eternity in the hearts of men; yet they cannot fathom what God has done from beginning to end." (Ecclesiastes 3:11) It is a powerful verse that fascinates me and makes me thankful that God in His Majesty loves me and cares for me.

The phrase "they cannot fathom" says that God cannot be completely understood, figured out, or grasped. He is much too complex for our simple finite minds to comprehend His Bigness. The word fathom has three definitions: 1) nautical term to measure the depth of water; 2) to get to the bottom of; 3) to measure the depth of. It is that third definition that strikes me as significant in the Ecclesiastes verse, "to measure the depth of." No one can measure the depth of God!!

I decided to present my ideas on Ecclesiastes 3:11, but in addition to that, I asked six friends to tell me how big is God to them. How have they been impacted by the immensity of God, how have they experienced only in their finite human capacity some of the immensity, complexity, and infinity of God? The responses were so incredibly inspiring and faith-searching that my husband Joe remarked that I should write a book and have friends, family, and associates present their personal interpretations of the Bigness of God. And so, that is how this book originated.

Every response has been truly personal and unique, each inspiring and encouraging. Everyone sees God's greatness in different ways, and each response shows a strong faith and the dependence upon a powerful and loving God. I hope that you will enjoy the beautiful and encouraging stories, sometimes heart-wrenching, and see how each has been touched by the greatness of God.

God's character gives us some inkling of His greatness: Omnipotent (all powerful), Omniscient (all knowing), Infinite, Almighty, Most High, Creator, and others. We are none of those things, and yet, we think we can know everything there is to know about God. We think that if we read a few books about God, or read through the Bible a few times, that we then are very knowledgeable about the Divinity of God. We can only scratch the surface of what there is to know about Him.

Let me give you an example of the Bigness of God to demonstrate that we can never fully comprehend God. A few years ago, I was reading a book by Francis Chan, a Christian author and minister. Chan referred me to YouTube to watch a three-minute video called "The Awe Factor of God," in which the visual begins at Chan's location in California and then zooms above the earth to show the curvature of the earth, what you would see if you were atop Mt. Everest. The picture zooms farther above the earth 100,000 kilometers, one-quarter the distance to the moon. Next, the visual zooms beyond the Sun, then to ten light years away, and the Sun is just a spot of light. We see the Milky Way Galaxy, then to 10-million light years, then beyond to clusters of galaxies, then we move to 100 million light years away, and we cannot see the Milky Way Galaxy anymore. And, we cannot see what is beyond that! OK, God created all that from nothing; He created the heavens and the earth and the entire universe, and we cannot see the end of it, then how BIG is God? Do you see what I am saying? He must be bigger than His creation, and yet, we cannot see the end of His creation. He is beyond our imaginings, beyond anything that we can perceive!

This book includes stories and perceptions of many who experienced situations, often when they were at their lowest, and who felt the presence of the Almighty God and saw their lives impacted by the touch of God. How could they possibly understand all the significance of that engagement with God? They did feel a change in their view of God, and thus, they felt a personal connection with the God of the universe. They knew that God had communicated with them in a very intimate way to show them that He truly cares for them and knows everything about them. I believe that you will find the stories encouraging so that you will want to know more about our loving and caring Creator.

The format of the book is simple to follow. The writer is identified in bold face and credentials follow. Then in italics, I present my personal view/feelings for each person to give you a little background of the person who wrote the piece. A title is given for the story, and then the story itself, sometimes short, sometimes more lengthy. Each person shares a favorite Bible verse that has a special connection for him or her. I myself present a verse for the writer based on the story he has written, or I may deviate and choose a verse that reminds me of the friend.

I have several suggestions on how this book can be used:

❖ It obviously can be a devotional, reading only one story each day, and then meditating on its lessons and applications.

❖ Some may wish to simply read it as one reads a novel.

❖ Some readers may find it helpful to select the Bible verses that connect with them and to memorize those verses for personal use.

❖ Some may make a list of all the ways we see God to discover a bigger picture of our Creator.

❖ Some readers may use the book to share with friends to encourage a stronger faith.

I have been led to write and compile this book, but ultimately God's purpose may be to make the readers be more aware of His presence and His intervention in their lives.

Can you fathom the mysteries of God?
Can you probe the limits of the Almighty?
They are higher than the heavens—what can you do?
They are deeper than the depths of the grave—what
can you know?
Their measure is longer than the earth
And wider than the sea.

(Job 11:7-9)

Oh, the depth of the riches of the wisdom and
knowledge of God!
How unsearchable his judgments,
and his paths beyond tracing out!
Who has known the mind of the Lord?
Or who has been his counselor?
Who has ever given to God,
that God should repay him?
For from and through him
and to him are all things.
To him be the glory forever!
Amen.

(Romans 11:33-36)

Brad Gaines, Managing Partner of Reset Strategies, Best-selling Author of Stand Apart, Louisville, KY.

Brad is very friendly and outgoing, always ready to serve. His is the dynamic young face of the marketing revolution. He commands immediate respect and trust. This story shows his personal love and concern for his family.

Kidnapped By Cancer...
Ransomed By Glory

On June 30, 2011, my first daughter was born. I think Dorothy Day (an American journalist) summed the feeling of that day the best way I've ever read. She said, "If I had written the greatest book, composed the greatest symphony, painted the most beautiful painting or carved the most exquisite figure I could not have felt the more exalted creator than I did when they placed my child in my arms for the first time."

Fast forward just three years to March 27, 2015. That was the day I held a cancer stricken daughter. That was the day our three year old daughter Adley was diagnosed with a rare form of pediatric cancer called neuroblastoma. Stage 4. Grave concerns abound. That was the day our daughter was kidnapped by cancer, abducted from a normal three year old life, and held hostage by the assailant of cancer.

In 2009, I was watching a movie titled "Gifted Hands," the true story about Dr. Ben Carson and the first ever surgery to separate twins conjoined at the head when a commercial for St. Jude Children's Research hospital in Memphis, TN aired asking for donations to help cure cancer stricken children. My heart was moved that day and I still remember thinking, as I logged online to their website to set up automatic financial donations, how awful that must be for those children and their families?

As a contributor to St Jude, every month I received patient spotlight updates about cure rates, stories about children overcoming the odds, and news about the overall fight against childhood cancer. Then I would throw the correspondence in the trash while shaking my head and saying, "I don't know what I would do if this was my family."

Little did I know that six years later, it would be my family. My own daughter would become a patient spotlight and we would be cancer parents.

My daughter's cancer was in her neck. Data showed less than 1% of children ever had neuroblastoma cancer in the neck. It looked like someone tried to poke a golf ball out the right side of her neck. Because of the placement of the tumor, clenching all life vessels in her neck, we wanted only the best surgeon to operate on her if the treatment plan was able to reduce the size to operable conditions.

It was then that St. Jude entered my mind, but it was six hours away, and the treatment plan was a year. My wife and I struggled under a "death clock" to determine whether to give her treatment at our home hospital or at St. Jude. We prayed for guidance. In a matter of minutes my phone rang and it was a Memphis phone number. "Hello, this is Brad." Caller: "Hello, Brad. This is Dr. Klosky. I was the best man in your cousin's wedding, and she called me and told me about your daughter Adley. I'm one of the attending physicians at St. Jude Hospital." I was stunned, shocked, chilled to the bone. I get chills as I relive it on these pages. "Brad, your home hospital will give Adley great care, but if you consider other alternatives we would love to help you. We have the #1 neuroblastoma surgeon IN THE WORLD here. I can arrange a transfer with the doctors there if you put me in touch with them." Six years ago I became a financial contributor to St. Jude, and now I was going to see where my money had been spent.

On Easter Sunday of 2015, my wife, daughter, and mother-in-law made a 400 mile drive to St. Jude Hospital where we would live for the next 5 months.

On one of the rare days Adley was able to go outside during her first two rounds of treatment, there was a gentleman who was repainting the gold paint on the dome of the Danny Thomas Pavilion. He saw Adley in her stroller and asked if she would like a piece of gold. He took a piece of wax paper and placed a square of gold foil paint inside it and gave it to her. Upon returning to the room, my wife placed it randomly in her Bible without thought.

A couple of months had passed since that day, and Adley was due to receive imaging scans to determine if her tumor had shrunk. The night before her scans, one of my wife's prayer warriors, who was known to send Scripture to her ever so often, sent in the middle of the night a recommendation via text to read Psalm 84, verse 7. When my wife opened up her Bible to read the verse, guess where that piece of gold was? You got it: on the page of that Scripture! There are over 2,170 pages in my wife's Bible. The Scripture reads, "They go from strength to strength (increasing in victorious power), till each appears before God in Zion." That verse was explained to me as when we see our strength is in God, the difficult places in life can be turned into blessings, the valleys of weeping can be turned into springs.

We received the news a week later that Adley had a perfectly normal scan. Praise God.

As part of Adley's year long treatment she underwent surgery to remove the lymph nodes once threatened by the growth. We were told that surgery would last many hours and to prepare for a full day. The surgeons had advised us that the reason it would take so long is that they typically have to go in and scrape the area to try and remove any area of risk. "It is like scraping gum from hot pavement," they said. That morning of the surgery, as we prayed, my father-in-law prayed, "Lord, just hand it over to them, Lord," making reference to the shrunken tumor area being easy to remove. I didn't know what to think when the surgeons walked out in under three hours. I walked briskly up to the surgeons, and after getting a "she's in recovery and doing fine report," I asked them what changed and why it took only a little under three hours. The surgeon looked at me and said, "The tumor was was just lying there, right on top." Praise God.

Today, our daughter is a healthy and cancer-free five year old...all because of our big God!

Brad's verse: Do not be anxious about anything, but in everything, by prayer and petition, with thanksgiving, present your requests to God. And the peace of God, which transcends all understanding, will guard your hearts and your minds in Christ Jesus. (Philippians 4:6-7)

My verse for Brad: Praise be to the God and Father of our Lord Jesus Christ, who has blessed us in the heavenly realms with every spiritual blessing in Christ. (Ephesians 1:3)

Joyce Oglesby, Author, Speaker, Radio Talk Show Host of Just Ask Joyce Show, Corydon, IN

She does everything for the glory of God, literally! She is the consummate multi-tasker, always has time for something else. She has overcome many obstacles, and she is God-focused and always has a new charity that she works very hard to be of service. Today she hosts a Christian radio talk show and enjoys life as a pastor's wife.

PERSEVERANCE DEEP WITHIN ME

When I was twelve years old, I pleaded with God, "Lord, please send me someone to teach me how to love." That was the heart of an abused child. Wrought with emotional, verbal, physical, and sexual abuse in the home of a highly dysfunctional family, I was grasping for answers of why I wasn't "suitable" to be loved. My immaturity and brokenness had convinced my small heart that I was not fit for love, and certainly didn't know how. Why else would the very ones who should love me the most hurt me the worst?

The Gideon Bible that had been placed in my hand at an elementary chapel time was my only link to life and hope. As I read those pages underneath my covers by flashlight each night, God's redundant zeal for the pursuit of my heart kept me eager for a future time I could not imagine but for which He knew every detail. I was everything but beautiful to me. My parents even told me so. Dad called me the "Ugly Duckling" no one would want. Mother told me repeatedly, "Don't worry that you're ugly; beauty is in the eye of the beholder." They both impressed upon me I wasn't "worth a hill of beans." Those comments and others could scar a tender heart and mind with negative impacts for a lifetime.

But once I began reading verses like 2 Samuel 22:20 and Psalm 18:19, "He brought me out into a spacious place; He rescued me because He delighted in me" and Ecclesiastes 3:11, "He has made everything beautiful in its time. He has also set eternity in the hearts of men, yet they cannot fathom what God has done from beginning to end." Those words swept hope all over my scarred-up life. I boldly asked the Gideons for His "big" Bible; I didn't settle for the little New Testament and Psalms version. I'm glad I found my voice!

Knowing that at five years old I had been compromised sexually, recalling that my mother was told by the hometown doctor, "Lola, someone is hurting your little girl and it needs to stop," and realizing she didn't know how and wasn't going to stop it, left me a helpless case. But I was not hopeless!

For seven long years, I prayed that prayer for someone to teach me how to love. Abuse continued until I would graduate from high school. God hand-picked Webby Oglesby for me, and O

Lord, how the love keeps coming!

Part of my prayer would be that God would protect me from pregnancy by a family member, because I knew it would change the course of my life forever. He did! I would not get my menstrual cycle until two months before graduation. I didn't know then, but see clearly today, how the puzzle pieces He fit together from beginning to end would work to the glory of His Kingdom. I promised Him in that prayer that if He did protect me, I would serve Him until death. I have not stopped and pray He fills me with the same kind of zeal to pursue others as was the zeal for which He pursued me.

I cannot begin to fathom why He loves me so. I only know without Him, I would perhaps have shared the lifestyle of my siblings or the many addicts and victims of life's dysfunctions. There is a perseverance deep within me that I cannot explain save for the love Christ Jesus exampled for me. Someone "did" teach me how to love. Yes, Webby, but before him, Christ Jesus was my Teacher…and I applied the knowledge through the loving arms of Webby. God is good. He knows it all. He has a plan for everyone who will submit to His good, pleasing, and perfect will. I am so thankful that I surrendered to Jesus early in my life. It has made for a "beautiful everything in time."

Joyce's verse: He brought me out into a spacious place; he rescued me because he delighted in me. (2 Samuel 22:20)

My verse for Joyce: You intended to harm me, but God intended it for good to accomplish what is now being done, the saving of many lives. (Genesis 50:20)

Pat Day, Past President of the Jockey's Guild, Mom's Closet Resource Center, The Kentucky Race Track Chaplaincy. Served on Kentucky Horse Racing Commission. Member of Racing Hall of Fame, Colorado Sports Hall of Fame, Kentucky Athletic Hall of Fame and National Wrestling Hall of Fame. Retired Thoroughbred Jockey and full time husband, father, and evangelist, Louisville, KY

Pat's racing career scanned four decades, and he rode more than 8,800 winners, including The Kentucky Derby, The Preakness, and The Belmont. Retired from racing, he is now an ambassador to the Race Track Chaplaincy, serving the spiritual needs of those who work behind the scenes at race tracks throughout the country. He openly and joyfully shares his faith.

DESIRE OF OUR HEARTS

My wife Sheila and I had been married for 5 years when I had an encounter with Jesus Christ in a hotel room in Miami, Florida, January 27, 1984, and became Born Again. On September 15, 1985, at the first service of a revival at Arlington Heights Assembly of God,

Sheila responded to the altar call and accepted Jesus Christ as her personal Lord and Savior. We have been jointly serving our Lord since then and are avid students of the Bible, believing it to be the inspired, infallible Word of God. If God said it, we believe it, and that settles it.

Shortly after this we began dreaming of starting our family. Because of female problems Sheila had suffered as a young girl, we knew it would be difficult to have children, but we were praying and standing on the promises of our great and awesome God, especially the promise of Psalm 37:4, "Delight yourself in the Lord and he will give you the desires of your heart." We exhausted all avenues available to us and were not able to conceive but continued to pray and believe that our God was able and that it would come to pass.

On Saturday, February 28, 1987, we arrived home cold and tired after a long day at the races at Oaklawn Park in Hot Springs, Arkansas, and had a message awaiting us from Chaplain Mike Spencer. When I returned his call, he asked if we could come to his house as he had something important he wanted to share with us. At first I tried to put him off, but he persisted and so we went. When we arrived, there was a bit of small talk, and then he told us that an OB/GYN had shared with him about a young lady who was with child but wanted to put the baby up for adoption. This doctor was a Born Again Christian and had been praying for the family that could adopt this child and give it a loving home. He had met us at a social function a few nights earlier. He had no idea we were trying to have a baby, but the Lord had impressed upon him that we were the couple.

Now we had never considered adoption, and so this possibility was a bit overwhelming to say the least. We all fell to our knees and prayed. Sheila and I went home and continued to pray as our emotions went from overjoyed to scared to death. The next day I was scheduled to ride a race in California, and I recall clearly that the entire plane trip, going and returning, was spent in prayer asking God to confirm to us that this was from Him. Sheila picked me up at the airport the following morning, and at first there was very little conversation when she suddenly stated, "I am going to put the baby seat in the middle!" "What?" I asked. "I am going to put the baby seat in the middle. You never know what side you might get hit on, and the baby will be best protected in the middle!" Needless to say it was non-stop chatter with a fair amount of "Thank you, Jesus" and "Hallelujahs!" for the trip home.

We immediately called Mike, who called the doctor, who informed him that the baby was due on Thursday. Arrangements were made to meet with a lawyer the next morning to file the necessary paperwork. We were setting waiting patiently in his office when he walked in and informed us that the doctor had been wrong on the birth date as the woman was in labor. (We didn't know at that time what sex the baby was, or the race, or anything else for that matter. We just knew it was a gift from our great and awesome God.) Our beautiful daughter Irene was born on March 3 and was lovingly placed in Sheila's arms on March 5, five days to parenthood! A miracle of miracles and joy unspeakable as once again our God was faithful, and we received "THE DESIRE OF OUR HEARTS!"

Pat's verse: May the God of hope fill you with all joy and peace as you trust in him, so that you may overflow with hope by the power of the Holy Spirit. (Romans 15:13)

My verse for Pat: Come and see what God has done, how awesome his works in man's behalf! (Psalm 66:5)

Stephen Tweed, CSP, Healthcare and Business Strategist, Professional Speaker, Leading Home Care, a Tweed Jeffries Company, Louisville, KY

Stephen is a good friend, and he is amazingly gifted in business and his personal achievements. He is quiet and reserved, and he has a depth of caring and compassion that is beyond the average. He is athletic and quite the sportsman. Everyone wants a friend like Stephen.

NOT DONE YET

It was an overcast day in October of 1971. We walked into the office of a world renowned pediatric neurologist in Pittsburgh, Pennsylvania. It was a dark gloomy office, but then he was a dark gloomy doctor. "You've been at Children's Hospital for ten days," he began. "I've run all the tests I know how to run. I'm not 100% sure, but I believe your one-year-old son has a rare neuromuscular disease called Werdnig-Hoffman Syndrome, Anterior Spinal Muscular Atrophy. This disease is very, very rare. I've been practicing medicine here for

30 years, and I have seen only twelve cases. I have no idea what causes it. There is no known cure. I believe your son will probably live to be three or four. Take him home and love him."

Take him home and love him. That's all.

Well, back then we did what the doctor ordered. So we took him home and loved him. And it worked. Jason got to be three, and then four. And then he got to be six, and went to elementary school. We did what most parents would do and tried our best to make sure Jason got a good education. He finished elementary school and moved on into middle school.

At age twelve, Jason developed severe scoliosis of the spine. His doctor was concerned that this curvature was causing pressure on some of his internal organs, so he referred us to Cleveland Clinic. We spent 21 days living in the Ronald McDonald House while an amazing orthopedic surgeon Jack Andrish opened Jason's back, fused all of the vertebrae together, and inserted two steel rods. During the recovery process, Dr. Andrish suggested we see another pediatric neurologist to get a new opinion and some new information about Werdnig-Hoffman.

The new doctor gave us new hope. He ordered an electric wheel chair for Jason, and suggested that we begin to think about the future. No one had ever said that before. Think about the future? (He was only going to live to be three or four! He's twelve!) Every day is a miracle.

Jason spent the next six months in a hospital bed in our dining room. He couldn't do much but read, watch TV, and play Atari. He got pretty good at using his frail hands to run the joy stick on the Atari game system. After he recovered enough to get out of his hospital bed, we went back to Cleveland to the electric wheel chair store. We looked at a number of chairs, and Jason picked the one he liked best.

The salesman in the store suggested that he try it out. We lifted Jason into the chair. The clerk turned the speed dial all the way down, and showed Jason how to use the joy stick. Jason reached down, turned up the speed dial, and zoomed off down the aisle at full speed. Playing Atari had some benefits; he already knew how to drive his wheel chair.

Over the next several weeks, Jason gained a whole new level of independence using his new electric wheel chair. One evening I came home from the office expecting to see a driveway full of kids because our house was often the gathering spot for the neighbor children. They all loved Jason and would come over to play. But this evening the driveway was empty. Our two daughters were in the living room; one doing homework and the other watching TV.

"Where's Jason?" I asked.

"He's right outside playing with the other kids," they said.

I went outside, but no Jason. I walked across the street to the neighbors, but they had not seen him. I called down the street. "Jason!" No Answer.

Have you ever had that happen? Your children disappear, and you don't know where they are. You begin to imagine all the things that could have happened. Well, imagine this situation. Here is a 12 year old who has never been out of sight of his parents or grandparents, and now he's gone.

I got on the phone and called a few friends, but no one had seen him.

Then, after about an hour, I looked up the street, and there came Jason rolling home in his new electric wheel chair. If you are a parent, you have mixed emotions. On one hand, you want to grab him by the shirt and shout, "Jason, Where have you been!?" On the other hand, you want to hug him and say softly "Jason, where have you been? I was worried about you." I can't remember now if it was the angry dad or the loving father. You can decide.

I said, "Jason, where have you been?" He said, "I was outside playing, and the other kids had to go in for dinner. Mom didn't have dinner ready yet, so I decided to go for a walk."

"I decided to go for a walk." This is a young man who has never taken a step in his life, but he went for a walk.

Well, Jason continued to go for a walk through life. He went on to high school, and graduated at the end of the eleventh year. He went on to college and graduated after three and a half years. And he came home to live with Dad.

By then I was single, having been dismissed from a long-term marriage. Jason and I made a home in our bachelor pad. Since I was in my own business as a professional speaker and consultant serving the home health care industry, we decided we needed some home care for Jason. I was traveling a lot, and we needed someone to come in and care for Jason while I was gone. That worked amazingly well, and Jason learned to live independently with the help of his caregivers.

In the meantime, I was at the National Speakers Association convention in Atlanta and met a fellow speaker from Louisville, KY. I was working with a hospital in Louisville at the time, so we arranged to meet for a light bite to eat after my leadership retreat with the hospital executives. That light bite turned into a few phone calls, another dinner, and a long distance relationship that led to marriage to an amazing woman. (How big is your God?) When I married Elizabeth, we decided to make our home in Louisville, Kentucky, 600 miles from where Jason and I were living in Reading, Pennsylvania.

After much consideration and research, Jason decided to stay in Pennsylvania. He kept the condo we were living in, took in a roommate to help him at night, and continued to receive the services of a local home care company. While it was pretty scary for both of us, GOD knew what He was doing: Jason learned to live independently. He met a young woman at a family Thanksgiving gathering, and they began to write to each other.

A year later they were dating, and then they decided to marry. For me it was amazing that Jason found a good Christian woman who loved him and wanted to marry him. Not so much for her parents. You can imagine their feelings when their oldest daughter announced she was marrying a young man who was totally disabled and lives in a wheel chair. Over time, Kristen's family came to know and love Jason as well.

Today is Jason's 46th birthday, forty-two bonus years and still counting. He is married, owns a home, owns his own internet marketing company, and has twins that just turned 14. He is a husband, a father, and a business owner. His physical ability is limited to using his right hand to operate the track ball on his computer and run his wheel chair.

In spite of those physical limitations, Jason has been blessed with intelligence, a sense of humor, and an amazing ability to communicate. He is fun to be around, and his clients love him. He is a great husband and a great dad.

We have learned that when God takes away some ability, He replaces it with extra ability in other areas. HE's not done with Jason yet. We don't know what HE has in store. Only HE knows.

How big is our GOD? He's huge. Over the past 46 years, we have prayed a lot for Jason and his family. God has answered some of our prayers, not all of them, but some of them. Why? Only God knows. You have all had experiences where you prayed for the healing of a loved one. God answers prayers in many different ways. Sometimes he heals the sick person. Sometimes he keeps the person alive, but in a state of "different-ability." Sometimes the person dies early. Who knows?

Only God could take the devastating diagnosis of Werdnig-Hoffman Syndrome and turn it into a life of service and inspiration. Over the years, Jason has used his experience with this disease to counsel and console families of other children. He has guided young people in navigating the world of disabilities. He wrote a book on "Colleges That Enable" to help students find a place to get an education in spite of their disability. He inspired his classmates and personal care attendants at college with his strength, his will power, and his sense of humor.

"He will probably live to be three or four. Take him home and love him." And 46 years later, we are still loving him. God had a purpose in creating Jason, and He's not done yet. How big is YOUR God?

Stephen's verse: Then little children were brought to Jesus for him to place his hands on them and pray for them. But the disciples rebuked those who brought them. Jesus said, "Let the little children come to me, and do not hinder them, for the kingdom of heaven belongs to such as these." (Mathew 19:13-14)

My verse for Stephen: Jesus replied, "You do not realize now what I am doing, but later you will understand." (John 13:7)

Cassie Soete, Marriage Mentoring Ministry over 25 years, Southeast Christian Church, Louisville, KY

Cassie is a very good friend, and we were born on the very same day, same year. Imagine! She and her husband have been extremely instrumental in saving many, many marriages. This is how it all began.

MY AWESOME GOD

Until death do us part…that's the beautiful promise George and I vowed the day we married on September 7, 1964. A marriage can certainly have its share of ups and downs, and ours was no exception.

On our 20th anniversary, my George informed me that he was leaving me to marry someone else, a close friend. There are no words to describe the devastation I felt! I felt numb on the one hand and totally out of control on the other hand. I thought I was going to die. I was faced with raising our six children without a full-time dad to help. The children were 2, 4, 13, 15,

17, and 19 years old at the time. All of my dreams of growing old with George were over, or so it seemed!

Being a very strong-willed person, (which can be good if channeled in the right direction), I began my mission to win my husband back. I tried everything imaginable, but nothing worked. In fact, things got worse! I prayed unceasingly, and then prayed even more. For four and a half years, George came in and out of our lives eight times, each time pledging that he was home for good. I grew wearier with each passing good-bye.

Around the four year mark, I lost all hope of restoration, and I remember being so angry with God. I was falling apart. One day I found myself on the floor screaming at God, "If You want this marriage to work, You will have to figure it out because I am finished!" It was a relief on my part, and I am quite sure the good Lord was glad I quit trying to do His job! That was the beginning of the total strength I found in my awesome God. I knew He would never leave me or forsake me, and He didn't. My prayers were working on me!

My faith became immovable with every step I took, with every breath I breathed. Philippians 4:13, "I can do everything through him who gives me strength" became a promise I still rely on every day of my life.

I told George he would have to earn his divorce every step of the way because my "death do us part" vow would not be broken on my account. I planned to be obedient to my God in spite of how I felt. It made George accountable for the first time in his life.

George began to see the changes in me and how my faith was an integral part of my life. In fact, one day George heard something I was saying about Jesus, and he said, "I want what you have," meaning my faith. One night while George was unable to sleep in his apartment, he reached for the Bible that the children and I had given him for Christmas one year. He was so convicted that he asked the Lord to come into his life. He never once looked back. He became a true servant to our Almighty God!

My faithful, awesome God restored our broken marriage to the fullest! I believe He did so, in part, because of my obedience to Him. I never dreamed our marriage would be so wonderful, an unbelievable, redeeming love story that surpasses any romance novel. Our loving, giving God became the center of our marriage, such an amazing 50 plus years to spend with the love of my life. My life is more complete because of my journey with George and my faith is so strong for the very same reason.

God showed His power by reuniting two broken souls to help others heal their marriages. We used our brokenness to start a marriage mentoring ministry and have helped countless couples to overcome adversity by being obedient to God even when times are tough.

My life has changed again: My precious George went to be with the Lord on April 7, 2015. I am blessed to have shared 18,462 days with my sweet, sweet husband. (just not enough!)

I see after one year of being alone that God continues to be my awesome God. He lifts me up even now as I write these very difficult words. But as usual, He has never left my side. It is the HOPE that I cling to as the children and I grieve the loss of such a godly man. I ache from missing him…now in "death we do part."

Cassie's verse: Come to me all you who are weary and burdened, and I will give you rest. (Matthew 11:28)

My verse for Cassie: Let us hold unswervingly to the hope we profess, for he who promised is faithful. (Hebrews 10:23)

Joe Bonura, CSP, Author, and National Speaker, Sales and Marketing, Louisville, KY

He is my husband and best friend, my biggest supporter. He owned a very successful advertising agency for seventeen years, and then became a national speaker. He exceeds at everything he does and still remains very humble about his accomplishments. He is an amazing dad to our three children. God gave me the best!

GOD TO THE RESCUE

On vacation in Boston, Massachusetts, my wife Carol and I were focused on kicking back and having a relaxing and historically educational experience. The TV networks reported that a hurricane was headed for the Gulf Coast.

We were not concerned because we heard that report many times over the years; however, our attitude changed when the weather channel predicted that Hurricane Katrina was headed directly for my former home town of New Orleans. Suddenly, the entire focus of our vacation changed. When I called my sister Linda in New Orleans to check on the family, she informed me that Mom and Dad needed to be evacuated from the senior living community where they were living. My mother was 83, and my dad was 87 years old. Mom was receiving hospice care, and she was bedridden, so she could not be moved without a special ambulance. With all the chaos throughout the city, the ambulance service was not responding to the calls of my brother-in-law Walter. Walter and Linda had to consider their own evacuation plans, as well.

I took over the task of evacuating Mom and Dad, and I called the ambulance service. After many attempts, I spoke with a very busy dispatcher who understandably acted as if she did not have time to speak with me. My first question was framed to recognize her dilemma and to show genuine empathy, "It sounds like you are up to your ears in alligators. I don't think that I would like to be in your position, and I appreciate your taking my call." She commented, "Thanks for noticing." I quickly explained the situation with my mom and dad.

She responded, "I'm sure that you can understand that we are doing everything we can to get to everyone in need, and I can assure you that we will make every effort to pick up your mom and dad as soon as possible." Understanding her situation, I said, "I can hear by the tone of your voice that you will do just that. I want to thank you in advance for your help in treating my mom as if she were your own mother." Within two hours, they picked up Mom and Dad and evacuated them to East Jefferson Hospital. I know the Holy Spirit was gently guiding me through that conversation.

The usual routine after hurricane evacuation was to sit out the storm, wait a few days until things settle down, and then head home—not this time. Three days later, my parents were still on the sixth floor of East Jefferson Hospital. The hospital was on auxiliary power, and there were total blackouts every few hours in order to conserve power. The first floor of the hospital was flooded, communications were down, and food was rationed because supplies were not being delivered. After hearing the news reports, I knew that we had to do something to get them out of the hospital to safer ground.

At 4:00am the next morning, in the lobby of the Boston Marriott Hotel, I was mind mapping to come up with a plan of action. It was then that I learned how big my God is. One thing was certain: my parents could not evacuate in a land vehicle; they needed a helicopter and so did thousands of other people. I could not reach them personally, and they could not get out on their own. So I prayed earnestly for a helicopter. At 7:00am, I received a phone call from my oldest son Joe, and he told me that he was in contact with a family friend Tom E. who had flown his helicopter down from Louisville to New Orleans to help in the rescue operations. Tom had a helicopter and promised to do everything in his power to rescue my parents from their dilemma. (I ask you: was that luck or Divine intervention?)

So that I could coordinate the rescue attempt, I called Tom, and after many busy signals and failed attempts, I was able to speak with him. Tom required the GPS coordinates of the hospital, so I obtained them for him, but when he flew the helicopter over the hospital, he was waved off. The hospital would not clear him to land because they thought he was possibly bringing more evacuees into an already stretched system. We had to contact the hospital in some way to let them know that Tom was returning on Saturday because it was the last window of opportunity for him to make the rescue.

Again I prayed that we could at least get in touch with my dad so that he could let the hospital know what was going on. The next day, just hours before the last rescue attempt, I received a phone call from my youngest son Nick, who informed me that my dad had called on a satellite phone borrowed from a nurse who was visiting the hospital. I immediately called my dad and told him to be on the roof in two hours with my mother. (How did that happen?)

Two hours later, the helicopter rescued them from the roof of East Jefferson Hospital. As the nurse put my mother into the helicopter, she told Tom that my mother would not have lasted another day. (Praise God for saving her!)

My parents were evacuated to Gonzales, Louisiana, where Hospice of Baton Rouge gave them a place to stay until we arranged for them to come to Louisville in an air ambulance.

Mom passed away six months after joining us in Louisville. We felt truly blessed to share those last days with her. My dad passed away ten years after his incredible rescue from the ravages of Hurricane Katrina.

Sometimes we experience miraculous things in life that are impossible to call a coincidence. Throughout every situation, from getting the ambulance and helicopter, the GPS coordinates, the nurse's satellite phone, to the safe accommodations, my God was a BIG God, indeed! There is no way that I can take any of the credit for saving Mom and Dad. God raised them up on eagles' wings and flew them into our waiting arms.

Joe's verse: But those who hope in the LORD will renew their strength. They will soar on wings like eagles; they will run and not grow weary, they will walk and not be faint. (Isaiah 40:31)

My verse for Joe: Trust in the LORD with all your heart and lean not on your own understanding; in all your ways acknowledge him, and he will make your paths straight. (Proverbs 4:5-6)

Lisa Roederer, Precept Bible teacher, Louisville, KY

She is an amazing friend and Christian. She teaches Precept Bible Study in her home and has a very loyal following. She is intelligent and resourceful, and you can usually find her burrowing through a Christian resource volume, gathering information to provide insight for her classes. She is the consummate student and loyal friend.

THAT BABY BOY

The immensity of God is His plan of salvation. It totally overwhelms me each and every time I think about it. Only God could devise a plan that would "fit" everyone. To clothe His Son, to clothe Him in flesh, He who is Spirit, so that He would be fully man and truly God, will never cease to overwhelm, behoove, astound me. That, that Baby Boy, in the manger, was God, is so, so incredible. That the Father devised a plan whereby His Son could have real blood, for ME, for everyone who believes, is enormous. That, that Baby Boy, was the "Lamb of God who takes away sins of the world" will always arouse emotion that I can hardly describe. I fall prostrate in my heart in thanksgiving. And then to know that even our faith is a gift...and He gifted ME with faith...I can only fall to my knees in my heart and with head bowed and quietly say... "Thank you, Lord." Hebrews 2: 3 says *how can we neglect so great a salvation?* We must not.

Lisa's verse: The LORD your God is with you, he is mighty to save. He will take great delight in you, he will quiet you with his love, he will rejoice over you with singing. (Zephaniah 3:17)

My verse for Lisa: I know that my Redeemer lives, and that in the end he will stand upon the earth. And after my skin has been destroyed, yet in my flesh I will see God; I myself will see him with my own eyes—I, and not another. How my heart yearns within me. (Job 19:25)

Mike Graham, retired Pastor, Director of Administration, Southeast Christian Church, Louisville, Kentucky.

Mike is an amazing human being. He gave up a very lucrative career in Chicago for a church position in Louisville at a greatly reduced salary. He is extremely efficient and very capable, especially in financial matters. He has had many medical setbacks and has handled them with patience and grace.

RATHER HAVE JESUS

In May, 1988, on Memorial Day weekend, I awoke to find a one-inch, black and blue bruise going across the top of my head. I made an appointment with a Dermatologist to try to find out what was causing my halo. After biopsies of the infected area, the news came back that I had Lymphoma, a non-Hodgkins form of cancer. Life expectancy was six months due to the cell type.

I had recently resigned from my job in Chicago since I had been offered the position of Administrator at Southeast Christian Church in Louisville, Kentucky. Our house was up for sale, and we were looking for housing in Louisville. What a nightmare!

My wife Sharon and I were visibly shaken by the news, but we prayed that God would lead us through this adventure. Our faith was strong and we knew that He was in control.

The next mission was to tell the Elders at Southeast what was going on and seek their counsel. We had a meeting with them in Louisville in late July, and they said God is a God of love, and the job would be mine when I came to Louisville. That was not what I expected to hear from them since I would have only six months to work. On August 8, 1988, I reported for work at Southeast.

The church staff prayed for me and my wife and my son and daughter. The Elders prayed for me, as well as the entire church family. Most of those praying were people that I had never met. Then I heard that prayers were being lifted up all over the world. Medical tests continued, shunts were surgically implanted, chemo began, and I was exhausted. Hair began to disappear, hearing worsened, taste buds quit working, and smell was gone.

I felt horrible physically, but spiritually energized by the well-wishers and prayers. I fought, and God won the victory because the six months came and went, then the years followed. I was not healed, but the cancer had stopped growing, and now 28 years later, I am still kicking. I have retired from the church, but I do lots of volunteer work in teaching, counseling, and offering my services on a board of directors. We have a home Bible study that has been in existence for 25 years.

What can I say to you about the trouble you will have in years to come or even now? Here are lessons that I have learned:

- ❖ Trust God and stand firm no matter what comes at you.

- ❖ Keep your faith in all circumstances.

- ❖ Pray like you have never prayed before.

- ❖ Remember that you need some close people around who will support and advise you as a Christian.

- ❖ Understand as much as you can about the nature of your illness.

- ❖ Be sure that your doctor listens to you because YOU are in charge of your body.

- ❖ Keep a positive attitude; give God the glory.

- ❖ Be thankful in all circumstances.

- ❖ Don't become mean-spirited or feel victimized by the illness.

- ❖ Understand that you have a beautiful home in Heaven waiting for you that will be void of pain, suffering, tears, and evil.

Since my initial bout with the Lymphoma, three more cancers have become part of my existence. I try to take them in stride, turning them over to God and letting Him lead. For me, life is better that way, and I can concentrate on people rather than feeling sorry for myself. I ascribe to the song "I'd rather have Jesus than anything this world affords me."

Since my battle with Lymphoma, I have had the following:

- ❖ Brain cancer

- ❖ Skin cancer

- ❖ Squamous cell carcinoma

- ❖ Pneumonia

- ❖ MRSA infection five times

- ❖ Back surgery

- ❖ Strep A infection

- ❖ Atria Fibrillation

- ❖ Type 2 Diabetes

- ❖ Congestive heart failure

My doctor says that I am in good shape for the shape that I am in.

Mike's verse: And we know that in all things God works for the good of those who love him, who have been called according to his purpose. (Romans 8:28)

My verse for Mike: Our citizenship is in heaven. And we eagerly await a Savior from there, the Lord Jesus Christ, who, by the power that enables him to bring everything under his control, will transform our lowly bodies so that they will be like his glorious body. (Philippians 3:20-21)

Dave Stone, Pastor of Southeast Christian Church, Louisville, KY

He is pastor of a huge church, and yet he reaches out to each individual congregant as a personal friend. He knows many by name. His sermons are passionate, and often emotional; he feels his faith!! He has a playful spirit, and often injects humor in his message. He is blessed by God.

A PERSONAL GOD

I love when the Lord shows up so big you just cannot deny His presence. Many years ago I invited one of my best friends from high school to come down for our Easter Service. That year we were having our service at Freedom Hall here in Louisville, Kentucky as the Sanctuary at Southeast Christian could not hold all of the folks if we tried to have one large service. Well, we were expecting about 13,000 people, and while the church was so excited about the numbers, I knew it would most likely be intimidating to my out-of-town guests. I found out later that when my guests arrived, they found a seat up in the rafters somewhere. And my friend and his wife who hadn't been to church in years later told me how they honestly thought, "Oh brother, this is going to be so big and so impersonal." But they gave it a shot anyway. Since I was doing the Communion Meditation that morning, we set it up to meet them after the service was over. The plan was to go to lunch at my in-laws' house when the convention center cleared out.

But when our worship leader announced a "meet and greet" during the service and had everyone turn and introduce themselves to one another, as the Lord would have it, the first people my guests shook hands with were my in-laws. When they said they were visiting from Cincinnati, my in-laws asked their names, and then my father-in-law, said, "I think you might be eating lunch at our house today!" Out of all those thousands of folks, my friends (with God's help) had found the one family they were soon to have a connection with!

All of a sudden that huge room, filled with thousands, got a little bit smaller, and it changed their perception and receptivity to what took place the rest of the hour. They glimpsed the immensity of God that day, as did we. What a faith booster! They discovered that, not only is He a powerful God, but He is a personal one too.

Dave's verse: When they saw the courage of Peter and John and realized that they were unschooled, ordinary men, they were astonished and they took note that these men had been with Jesus. (Acts 4:13)

My verse for Dave: Not to us, O LORD, not to us but to your name be the glory, because of your love and faithfulness. (Psalm 115:1)

Liz Curtis Higgs, *New York Times* best-selling Author, Louisville, KY

Liz has one goal: to help women embrace the grace of God with joy and abandon. She is the author of 35 books with 4.6 million copies in print, including Bad Girls of the Bible and The Girl's Still Got It. Follow her online Bible study at LizCurtisHiggs.com.

LORD, I WANT TO BE INVISIBLE

As a conference speaker, I pray every time before I step on the platform. Sometimes I pray for strength, other times for energy, often for clarity of thought, and always for the guidance of the Holy Spirit.

One Saturday morning in Chicago I felt strongly led to pray, "Lord, I want to be invisible." When you're the one holding the microphone on a brightly lit stage in front of a thousand people, it's tricky *not* to be seen. But I knew that's what God wanted me to pray, and so I did, with a certain amount of fear and trembling.

When I speak today, help me disappear, Lord. Make it all about you and your Word and not at all about Lizzie and her words. Let them see only You on this stage. Amen.

Shortly after that silent prayer, I was introduced. Away I went, sharing a message about miracles from the story of Mary of Nazareth, focusing on the angel Gabriel's promise to her, "For with God nothing shall be impossible." (Luke 1:37 KJV)

Even though I was speaking straight from the heart, putting my whole self into my message, something wasn't working. I didn't feel a deep connection with the audience, didn't sense I'd captured their full attention, which wasn't their fault: it was mine.

Help, Lord! This is a prayer I've often sent heavenward in the middle of a presentation, but especially that day in Chicago. *Help!*

He answered my prayer at once, but not in the way I expected. The lights on the stage blinked out so quickly, the audience gasped. I could still see the women, but they couldn't see me. At all.

Then I laughed. Loudly. "Oh, my sisters! This is exactly what I prayed for earlier. 'Help me disappear, Lord. Let them see only You on this stage.' He did it, girls. He answered my prayer. Truly, with God nothing is impossible!"

Although I heard people backstage frantically trying to find a solution, I knew God had already done so. I was in the dark so that He could shine.

Breaking free from my notes and trusting God for the words, I moved closer to the edge of the stage, nearer still to the audience, and shared His message instead of mine. Do I recall what I said? I do not. I only remember the sheer *power* of His presence in that room. We all felt it, and quickly realized it had nothing to do with me and everything to do with God.

When our time together came to a close, I offered the women before me His gift of salvation. The chance to be washed clean, made whole, recreated anew in the image of His Son.

"Is the Lord calling you?" I asked. At that precise moment, a cell phone rang, close enough to the stage that my microphone picked up the sound. It was an old-school ring, making it sound even more like a phone call.

A thousand women exploded in laughter. I did too. God's presence was so palpable, we were all sure He was on the other end of the line!

God did far more than save my floundering presentation that day. He saved many of His daughters, welcoming them into His embrace. "Now to the King eternal, immortal, invisible, the only God, be honor and glory for ever and ever. Amen" (1 Timothy 1:17).

Liz's verse: Therefore, if anyone is in Christ, he is a new creation; the old has gone, the new has come! (2 Corinthians 5:17)

My verse for Liz: You love righteousness and hate wickedness; therefore God, your God, has set you above your companions by anointing you with the oil of joy. (Psalm 45:7)

Bob Russell, Retired Senior Pastor, Southeast Christian Church, Louisville, KY

He is a retired pastor of Southeast Christian Church, a mega-church of 21,000 people. Liked by everyone, he preached at Southeast for 40 years. He currently leads monthly mentoring retreats for pastors, guiding them in speaking and church matters. He is a frequent speaker at The Cove, a Christian retreat run by the Billy Graham Evangelistic organization. He also has a weekly blog on topical subjects called Bob Russell Ministries.

GOD'S WORD IS POWER

I saw the Bigness of God on a mission trip to Cuba a little over a decade ago. I was asked to speak at a house church which met under careful surveillance from the communist government.

When I arrived, I noticed that the people were jammed inside the home, and there was little space to move. I realized that a formal, structured sermon would not work in that situation, be-sides I was speaking through an interpreter and that makes ef-fective communication very difficult. So, I decided to give an impromptu message and just basically review the good news of the gospel.

I spoke for fifteen minutes and couldn't get a feel for how it was going over. The language and cultural barriers seemed ominous to me that night. When I was finished, I felt frustrated about my message, which seemed to me to be disjointed and pretty bland. I didn't sense that the people were resonating with my words at all. I felt a tremendous emptiness, and af-terward made my way to a little kitchen to escape the group.

I heard singing from the other room where the people were gathered. Then the pastor came into the kitchen to get me; he said, "Bob, come back to the room with us." Standing at the very front was a handful of people. I asked the pastor, "What do you want me to do?" A little impatient with my question, he responded, "You need to pray for them! They want to ac-cept Jesus."

It was then that I realized while I spoke the words, it is God who touches the hearts for the harvest. The power of the gos-pel was all that was needed. The Apostle Paul wrote, "My message and my preaching were not with wise and persua-sive words, but with a demonstration of the Spirit's power, so that your faith might not rest on human wisdom but on God's power." (1 Cor. 1: 4-5)

Bob's verse: Now to him who is able to do immeasurably more than all we ask or imagine, according to his power that is at work within us, to him be glory in the church and in Christ

Jesus throughout all generations, for ever and ever! Amen. (Ephesians 3:20-21)

My verse for Bob: Serve wholeheartedly, as if you were serving the Lord, not men. (Ephesians 6:7)

Naomi Rhode, CSP, CPAE, CPAE Hall of Fame, Past President National Speakers Assn., Past President Global Speakers Fdn., Co-Founder SmartHealth, Scottsdale, AZ

Naomi lives and breathes the spirit of love and kindness to everyone she meets. She is everyone's friend, and she is always happy and content. She and her husband Jim are part of our SoulJourners group of six that has been traveling together every year for 17 years.

THE GOD I WORSHIP!

When we try to contemplate the immensity of God… when we try to fathom His complexity… when we try to "handle" the foreverness of eternity… and when we realize, yes, He always was and we were with Him forever before, and will be with Him forever, after life, we are caught up in mind expanding, heart beating, explosive thinking about this God that we worship!

And, then, and then, and then…we are caught off guard that He really knows us personally, and this immense God lives within humans like me! And…He does!!

Having had two "near death experiences," I know deep within my knowing that this God was the one that gave me TOTAL PEACE.

Having been on a plane most weekends for 45 years, as a Professional Speaker, flying was usually the best time to read and to rest…no concerns, just watching the world go by below and thinking/praying about the privilege of speaking at Mackinac Hotel, in beautiful Mackinac Island.

This trip, however, was different. I had been sick the day before. A visit to the emergency room allayed my concerns temporarily, but the small plane from Chicago to Traverse City was a "rough ride," and the feelings of "I am not well" returned over and over as I tried to block them from my mind.

After landing, Jim went to get the luggage, as I was greeted by our host, a dear friend. He gave me a welcoming hug, and as I attempted to hug him back, my arm went limp, face fell, and leg collapsed….I said, "I think I am having a stroke"…and I was!

At one point in the ER, I felt myself lift off the bed. I was up near the ceiling, looking down on my body. Surreal indeed!!

Hmmm, is this what it is like to go to be with Jesus? Am I dying? (Which of course we really do not do if we are already dead. As believers, we close our eyes here and open them there with Him).

Providential it is! And…I am totally at peace…amazing!!

An Infinite God would care to be in this room with me.

An Infinite God would care to give me confidence.

Confidence in His presence, and giving me total peace!

I said to Him (because He WAS there), "Either take me to heaven, or let me down to live on earth. Either is fine with me. But, could you please stop the room from spinning?!

Slowly, slowly, I was lowered, by Him, to my body, my life, a loving husband, Jim, a mission "to take Christ into the marketplace...the secular world", my three children, and twelve grandchildren.

He is infinite, unfathomable, incomprehensible, so big, I am so small, yet He loves ME, lives in ME, knew ME before the foundations of the Earth, called ME, and has prepared eternity with Him for ME!

Yes....truly amazing, my God! Do you know Him?

Postscript: He is also an amazing Healer, restoring me to amazing health, to serve Him this past eight years and hopefully years, and years to come! I am praising Him who lives in me, yet reigns in the Heavens that He created! He is TRULY unfathomable!

Naomi's verse: For God did not give us a spirit of timidity, but a spirit of power, of love and of self-discipline. (2 Timothy 1:7)

My verse for Naomi: You will keep in perfect peace him whose mind is steadfast, because he trusts in you. Trust in the LORD forever, for the LORD, the LORD, is the Rock eternal. (Isaiah 26:3-4)

Dr. Willie Jolley, Author, Hall of Fame Speaker, Nationally Syndicated Radio Show host, Washington, DC

Willie is a dynamic speaker for the Lord. He speaks from the heart, and his words and actions always glorify the Lord. He has been blessed with an incredibly powerful singing voice, and he uses it in his speeches to the delight of his audiences.

TRUST ME

Ecclesiastes 3:11 reads, "He has made everything beautiful in its time. He has also set eternity in the hearts of men, yet they cannot fathom what God has done from beginning to end." I have found that this verse is absolutely true, especially when linked to Romans 8:28 which reads, "And we know, that in all things God works for good of those who love him, who have been called according to his purpose." These two verses give us insight into how faith works.... faith works by trusting in God, even when we don't understand what He is doing. We understand that His ways are not our ways! It is about learning to trust Him and to learn to continue to walk and move forward by faith, and not by our own sight or understanding.

My personal story is an example of learning to trust in God. I was a nightclub singer in Washington, DC. I built one of the top nightclub acts in the city. Things were going great. People would line up at 7 o'clock for the 8 o'clock show, and then another group would line up at 9 o'clock for the 10 o'clock show. We had standing room only shows and it was one of the most popular nightspots in DC. I won the Washington Area Music Association Award five times for best jazz singer and entertainer. Things were going great!

Then one night I came to the club, and the club manager said he wanted to have a meeting later that night. I told the guys in the band, "They finally want to talk! We've been selling out for months! We are about to get our raise!" I walked in his office that night, and he said, "You were great tonight! The people love you! We've made a lot of money since you've been here!" I said, "Yes! Yes! Yes!" I was primed and ready to talk about my raise! But that was when he dropped the bomb and said, "The owners of the club have decided to make a change. They love you and your band but they need to get a better return on investment, and the only way to get it with a full nightclub is to lower the costs, and you and your band are the highest costs. So they have decided to try something else that is filling up nightclubs around the country, yet is a lot cheaper than a band…they bought a Karaoke machine!" I was devastated! I couldn't believe my ears!

On my way home, I cried out to God and said, "Why did you make me a good singer and entertainer to have me get fired from the best gig I have ever had?" I couldn't understand why this was happening, yet a voice was speaking to my spirit with one line that repeated over and over again, "Trust me!"

Soon thereafter, I was offered a job with the Washington, DC Public Schools, who were looking for someone with a background in entertainment and also a degree in counseling, and I had both. I took the job, figuring I would just do this long enough to pay some bills while I worked on my next music gig. While working at the school system, my boss asked me to visit schools and talk to the students about staying away from drugs and violence. I told my boss I was not a speaker, but was a singer, but she said I had theological and counseling background and should be able to say something of worth, and so she sent me out and said, just do the best you can do.

I went to the school and spoke to the students, and it was fair but not a big success, so I then did what I was comfortable doing: I started singing and entertaining and mixed it with the speech…and at the end they gave me a standing ovation. The principal of the school told me that she was amazed because her kids were tough and never stood up for anyone. She immediately picked up the phone and called a principal at another school, and she recommended that the other principal have me come speak for her students. From there, more and more principals did the same thing, and I started getting invitations to speak every day, sometimes as many as five times per day.

After a year, I left and started my full time speaking business. Now, twenty-five years have gone by, and I have spoken all over the world, have been named "One of the Outstanding Five Speakers In The World," been inducted into the Speakers Hall of Fame, have one of the top rated inspirational radio shows in America and authored a number of bestselling inspirational books.

I learned that God's Word is true, that we cannot know what God is up to, and that as in Romans 8:28 "in all things God works for the good of those who love him, who have been called according to his purpose."

Finally, I want to share that this concept does not just impact you personally but God will prove that He can use you to work good for others as well. I was in church one Sunday, and we went to a different service than we regularly go to. I am an altar counselor at my church, and when the pastor gives the altar call, I am listed as one of the senior altar counselors. So that Sunday, when the pastor gave the altar call, I was standing waiting for the first person to come, yet when the person started on his way to meet me, a deacon jumped up and took his hand and took him to the altar. I was a little surprised because the deacons are the second in line for counseling. I couldn't quite understand why the deacon had jumped up, and at that moment, I felt that same line flowing through my spirit, "Trust me!" I waited and a few minutes later, a young teen came up the altar, and I shook his hand and told him I would be his counselor.

I went back to the counseling room with the young man, and he told me that he was a visitor and was only in the area because he had gone to a friend's birthday party, and the friend brought him to church. We talked about his faith, and he accepted Jesus as his Lord and Savior. Yet, he told me that he doubted if he would attend again because he lived a far distance from the church.

I told him I was glad he accepted the Lord, but it was also important to find a good church to attend. He said he lived in another part of Virginia, and he didn't live in an area long because his mother moved a lot because of her work, so it was hard to find a good church to attend. I told him I hoped he would be able to come back when he was in the area again. Then something amazing happened, that showed why I had not taken the first person to come forward at the altar call, but was told to wait. And in that waiting, I was reminded to "Trust Him!" Then the young man said, "We live in Virginia, but we often visit my grandmother on weekends, and she lives in DC." I asked him where she lived, and he said, "5741 Colorado Ave NW!" I looked to the sky and hollered, "Thank you, Lord! You did it again!" I then looked at the young man and said, "I live in the same block!" WOW! God continues to amaze me!

God truly works all things together for them that love Him and are called according to His purposes. He proved that His word is true, and that Ecclesiastes 3:11 is right on...that "He has made everything beautiful in its time. He has also set eternity in the hearts of men, yet they cannot fathom what God has done from beginning to end." AMEN!!!!

Willie's verse: Seek first his kingdom and his righteousness, and all these things will be given to you as well. (Matthew 6:33)

My verse for Willie: Whether you turn to the right or to the left, your ears will hear a voice behind you saying, "This is the way; walk in it." (Isaiah 30:21)

Dr. Nido Qubein, Author, Speaker, President of High Point University, High Point, NC

He is incredibly successful and so very sincere and generous. His life story is one of hard work and achieving goals. He is a recipient of the Horatio Alger Association for Distinguished Americans. He has received so many prestigious awards that it would take several pages to list them, and yet, he has never forgotten where he came from. God has blessed him richly.

ART OF THE POSSIBLE

As I struggled to improve my fluency of English in a tiny town where I hardly knew a soul, I knelt beside my bed and cried my eyes out. I had just found out that someone had covered my second year of tuition at Mount Olive Junior College. That person didn't know me; I didn't know them. I still don't. All I know is that person heard I needed help.

Right then, with hands clasped in prayer, I promised God Almighty that some day, I too would be a benefactor for struggling college students. I'll never forget that moment because it helped me understand even more the depth of God's love. In our lives, we always need moments like that. They anchor us. They anchored me.

I was the youngest of five, a son without a father in the Middle East. My father died following years of failing health when I was 6. After his death, our mother worked two jobs, day and night, to provide for us.

She had gone no farther in school than the fourth grade, but I believe she had earned an advanced degree in common sense. She instilled in me the values of life and timeless principles for living. She taught; I listened.

She knew education was my ticket to a better life. So, at age 17, with her blessing, I left my home with $50 in my pocket and came to America because I believed in the American Dream. In 1966, I traveled 7,000 miles away from my home to get an education in a land where I knew little about the tenor of the times and the folkways of the region. But in a place that felt so foreign to me at first, I didn't feel alone. I found love and compassion and hospitality.

I had a housemother named Verta Lawhon, a mannerly woman in her 60s who loved watching "The Lawrence Welk Show." I watched it with her!

Unknown to me, before I completed my second year, she slipped into my bank account enough money for me to buy a car. I had saved $375 from work. The next thing I knew, I had $750. She was a woman who earned only $100 a month. But she wanted to help me. When I asked her why, she told me she would rather invest her money in the life of a budding young man rather than deposit it in a bank account somewhere.

Then came the anonymous donor. He or she made me see first-hand how God works through people in all sorts of ways.

In 1973, right when I started my first business, I took $500 – all the money I had -- and started a scholarship to help college students like me. Years later, my family and friends started a foundation, and since then, we have granted millions of dollars to help hundreds of students go to college.

It's easier to help others when you're successful and have the resources. But no matter what our resources are, each of us has the ability to do amazing things. We all have been created for a purpose, and when our purpose is to help someone else discover their own purpose, magic happens. We become one. We become family. Verta Lawhon and my benefactor, a person I never had a chance to thank, helped me realize that.

With their help, I began my life. I went on to graduate from High Point College and the University of North Carolina-Greensboro, marry a wonderful woman, raise four wonderful children and start a life that took me around the world.

I have had a successful career as a speaker, author, executive consultant, leadership expert, and business entrepreneur. But I have always seen myself as an educator at heart, and in 2005, after years as a member of the school's board of trustees, I became president of my own alma mater: High Point University.

I have felt the ever-present hand of God guiding me in everything I have ever done, and no matter where I have been or what I have achieved, the kindness of others and my moment on bended knee nearly a half century ago have never been lost on me.

Those moments helped me become who I am today. A steward. A grateful citizen.

At High Point University, I tell our students to be mindful of their own life moments that can become turning points that can define who you are, who you become, and open your eyes to what I call the "art of the possible."

I'm reminded of that every time I step into our theater on campus and look up. Painted above the entrance are eight words from the Book of Luke, Chapter 12, Verse 48. It's my favorite Bible verse.

To whom much is given, much is required.

So much wisdom in so few words.

Nido's favorite verse: From everyone who has been given much, much will be demanded; and from the one who has been entrusted with much, much more will be asked. (Luke 12:48)

My verse for Nido: (May God) equip you with everything good for doing his will, and may he work in us what is pleasing to him, through Jesus Christ, to whom be glory for ever and ever. (Hebrews 13:21)

Phillip Van Hooser, MBA, CSP, CPAE, Professional Speaker, Trainer, Author and Leadership Authority, Founder of Leaders Ought To Know LLC, Princeton, KY

Phil is a past president of the National Speakers Association. He is warm and genuine and approachable. He is an achiever and a leader. A finer person you will never meet. His story is not exaggerated, and it is truly remarkable!

HELP MY UNBELIEF

It was late September, 2000, and the central Florida morning was a spectacular panoramic scene worthy of any "Visit Sunny Florida" post card. The grass was a lush emerald green, the sky a brilliant blue, the clouds puffy white. It was the type of day King David might have enjoyed as he wrote, *"This is the day the LORD has made; let us rejoice and be glad in it."* (Psalm 118:24)

But that day, as my eyes beheld the scene, its beauty went largely unnoticed. My heart was far from glad and in no mood to rejoice. As every Floridian knows too well, beautiful morning clouds can transform themselves into ferocious afternoon thunderstorms. Storm clouds were gathering on the horizon in my spirit.

Eighteen months earlier, I had been diagnosed with ulcerative colitis, an inflammatory bowel disease — with no known cure. From the moment of diagnosis, my doctor worked with me to control the rapid and precipitous decline in my health. But nothing worked. Just eighteen months earlier, I had been a healthy, active 43-year old. Now 50 pounds lighter, my health and vitality declined daily. The decision had to be made. My only hope was major surgery. In a few short weeks, I would undergo what my doctors called a "proctocolectomy with a J-pouch anastomosis," a two-part procedure. In layman's terms, my colon would be completely removed, accompanied by a resection of my small intestine, with an extended period of recuperation to follow.

I was troubled by the prospects of surgery, but even more troubled by the financial considerations associated with the impending surgery. This surgery would require up to five months of recovery time, longer if complications arose. My doctors candidly explained that work during recuperation was not an option. I was an entrepreneur, a small business owner, our family's sole provider. My wife and young children depended on me. I was deeply troubled.

As a believer, I recognized the importance of taking my every concern to the throne of grace and presenting them to my Lord. And I had. I had prayed fervently and repeatedly. I prayed for strength, courage, wisdom, restoration — and I prayed specifically for some way to make it financially — where there seemed to be no way. But I was much like the man who approached Jesus, asking Him to heal his son. Mark 9:23-24 records the interaction. *Jesus said, "Everything is possible for him who believes." Immediately the boy's father exclaimed, "I do believe; help me overcome my unbelief."*

I WAS that man! I believed the Lord can do all things. But in that moment, on that central Florida highway, my confidence was waning. I could only see menacing clouds, not beautiful skies. I needed help with my unbelief.

As I continued to drive, my cell phone rang — a corporate client calling. She got right to the point. "Phil, I need a favor. Our fiscal year is ending shortly, and I have unspent money in my training budget. I don't want to lose it, but our calendar simply will not allow me to schedule anymore training for at least six months. We have already decided to have you lead that future training. Phil, I've never done this before, but would you be willing to let us pay you what is left in the budget now, and then apply it later to training that we will schedule sometime next year?"

I couldn't believe what I was hearing. The amount in question was more than enough to provide financial security throughout my period of incapacitation. I gladly, joyously, and thankfully accepted her proposal.

Once again, the Lord was faithful in watching over one of His helpless children. And I learned again that God's timing is always perfect. He was there exactly when I needed Him most. And once again His Word became real in my life.

Phil's verse: Trust in the LORD with all your heart and lean not on your own understanding; in all your ways acknowledge him, and he will make your paths straight. (Proverbs 3:5-6)

My verse for Phil: My God will meet all your needs according to his glorious riches in Christ Jesus. (Philippians 4:19)

Glenna Salsbury, Author of The Art of the Fresh Start, Professional Speaker, Scottsdale, AZ

She is an incredible speaker and loves to be before Christian audiences that are hungry for the Lord. She has written several books and has a blog called Heavenly Treasures that gives insight into the Scriptures. She has won numerous prestigious awards in the National Speakers Association.

LONGING IN MY HEART

When I was between my junior and senior year at Northwestern University, I did a three-month study program at the American University in Mexico. I was not a Christian. I was a churchgoer, but I did not know the Lord.

One weekend a small group of us went to Acapulco for the weekend. We were on the beach late at night. It was pitch dark. I was lying on a towel on the sand, looking straight up into the velvet blue-black sky. The stars were twinkling like diamonds.

The Milky Way looked like someone had thrown a handful of jewels across the sky.

In one moment in time, a moment imprinted on my mind forever, I realized that Eternity existed, that God existed and that Heaven existed!!! That moment planted a deep longing in my heart to know about Eternity. It was an emotional longing…

In the next two years, miracles unfolded in my family. My parents came to know Christ at 54 years old, after years of serving in the church. Their fervor led me to study the Bible and research the scientific side of creation. The Lord brought me to see that He is indeed God and that I could know Him in Christ!!! He began planting the awareness of Eternity in my heart in Acapulco, Mexico—just by gazing at the heavens! And at 21 years old, my life was transformed!!!

Glenna's verse: I want to know Christ and the power of his resurrection and the fellowship of sharing in his sufferings, becoming like him in his death, and so, somehow, to attain to the resurrection from the dead. (Philippians 3:10)

My verse for Glenna: The heavens declare the glory of God; the skies proclaim the work of his hands. (Psalm 19:1)

Elizabeth Jeffries, CSP, CPAE, National Speaker, RN, Author, Louisville, KY

Elizabeth is my very dear friend. She is passionate about life and knows instinctively how to accomplish her goals. We travel with her and her husband Stephen and have some of the most memorable discussions about Jesus and about life. She is part of our family, for sure!

A PERSONAL MESS

Growing up in a traditional Italian Catholic family on the west side of Chicago, we never missed mass on Sunday. Most of my early life I went to mass and communion every day. We never talked about God in our family, and in fact, I don't remember many times we used the name "Jesus." It was understood that our faith was personal and just between me and God.

My early years were tough for me. My father had a serious alcohol problem, and my dear mother mainly focused on keeping the peace and keeping us out of his way. I was so different from my three siblings. Seems I was always searching for more of everything. I had dreams and goals and I spoke out and was curious and eager to explore the world! I was that strong-willed child of today. My siblings were quiet and obedient and never caused problems; I caused enough for all of us, which constantly rattled my controlling father who seemed to want to control everything, including me.

I believe I always knew Jesus. I prayed to him, felt His presence and protection in my unstable home life, and was continually comforted by Him. I didn't know Scripture except for what I heard at mass. I never opened a Bible myself until way into adulthood. It was just me and God. While I felt loved by Him, I also feared Him and lived many years with guilt and shame.

An unstable, inconsistent home life often leads to looking for love in all the wrong places. That country music song was written for me at that time because I fell right into that trap. Six desert years followed where I was spiritually and emotionally lost and alone. Confused and in deep emotional pain, I abandoned any semblance of faith in God that I had, making poor decisions and unwise choices, especially in relationships. Failed marriages, disappointments, and a broken heart many times over became the norm. Hungry for love and acceptance, in essence, I became the woman at the well.

In spite of those desert years emotionally and spiritually, I finished college, had great leadership and management jobs and eventually started my own business as a speaker and consultant and executive coach. After all, I messed up enough that I figured maybe I could save a few others from my mistakes!

It's true God works in mysterious ways even when we don't know He's working! About this time He introduced two precious Christian women into my life, Naomi Rhode and Liz Curtis Higgs, who loved me unconditionally and showed me what life in the Lord looks like. I didn't get it at first and had a hard time thinking differently and changing habits. Single, successful in my career, and stable financially, I was pretty independent and didn't trust many people.

Gradually, I knew I needed to clean up my life and fill that hole in my soul. And so I began my journey to Jesus. He became the Man I was looking for! I longed to know Him, really know Him! I knew so little and wanted to know so much. Naomi told me to do three things…study scripture, join a Bible based church, and cultivate Christian friends. Obedient (maybe for the first time in my life) I did what she told me to do. And so the Lord became number one in my life, and He started growing me.

Eventually I met a godly man who also wanted to know more of Jesus. Together we grew a friendship and a healthy relationship with Christ at the center. We married and then were baptized together, committing to a covenant with each other and Christ. Over the past 25 years we have been on an amazing faith journey which continues to fill us with deep joy in the Lord and sustain us through tough times.

Liz and Bill Higgs invited us to our very first Bible study in their home. For 18 months we studied the book of John in detail. I will never forget the moment when Bill read John 15:16. *You did not choose me, but I chose you and appointed you to go and bear fruit – fruit that will last.* And John 15:19 *...you* *do not belong to the world, but I have chosen you out of the world.*

I remember being stunned and that I could not stop the tears from flowing down my face! I wanted to fall on my knees but I could not move! *What? He CHOSE me! He CHOSE me! He chose ME? Nasty, wretched, prideful, sinful me! I can't get my mind around this! Why me? I am nothing! All the times I ignored Him, and He stayed by me and loved me anyway! What kind of God is this? I don't deserve His love. I will never deserve His love. Forgive me, Lord. Forgive me, please. I am so sorry. I love you so very much.*

In that memorable moment in 1995, I glimpsed the power and glory of Jesus Christ and experienced His immeasurable love and His gift of GRACE.

Thank you, Jesus! Thank you!

Elizabeth's verse: I can do everything through him who gives me strength. (Philippians 4:13)

My verse for Elizabeth: For the eyes of the LORD range throughout the earth to strengthen those whose hearts are fully committed to him. (2Chronicles 16:9)

Ty Yokum, Chick-fil-A Headquarters, Atlanta, GA

He is my brother, and he has a gift for the adventurous life. My children have adored him as their Uncle Ty. He has a heart for God and gives much of his free time to acting as chef to friends and associates. He prepares enormous Southern feasts (Cajun mostly) for parties and charges only his costs, and then kindly requests donations to his favorite charity, Grace for all, a children's center and ministry dedicated to serving the children of Ethiopia.

COME TO THE TABLE

It was a sunny day outside and the wind was blowing. I was doing laundry for my missions team and was watching the clothes dry as shirts, pants, and towels air dried on the makeshift clothes line (remember those days?). I was reading the book "Why Good People Do Bad Things" as I waited. Suddenly a very clear thought came to me, so clear that I could swear someone was talking with me. "YOU have some dirty laundry, you know. It's time to clean it up." It was not a slapin-the-face kind of thought, but, more of a loving, caring, you-need-to-know-this kind of thing. I sat there initially, ashamed and convicted. The shame was self-imposed, but the conviction was spiritual.

In that short moment, I felt HIS presence, experienced HIS awe and wonder, could not fathom HIS immensity, and yet, was enveloped by HIS love. HE didn't lecture me. HE didn't shame me. HE didn't chastise me. HE only loved me. HE loved me enough to make me aware of the sin in my life that took me further away from HIM. HE offered me encouragement, hope, love, but more importantly, a relationship with HIM, God Almighty, Creator of the universe, Maker of all men, the unfathomable God. How blessed I was, and still am, to be invited to the table with HIM.

Ty's verse: Therefore, I urge you, brothers, in view of God's mercy, to offer your bodies as living sacrifices, holy and pleasing to God—this is your spiritual act of worship. Do not conform any longer to the pattern of this world, but be transformed by the renewing of your mind. Then you will be able to test and approve what God's will is—his good, pleasing, and perfect will. (Romans 12:1-2)

My verse for Ty: God is our refuge and strength, an ever-present help in trouble. (Psalm 46:1)

Katherine Magnuson, High School Latin Teacher, Christian Academy, Louisville, KY

Katherine is a powerful Christian, and she works in the perfect place for her: among young students who can see her example and can be influenced by her strong faith. She and her husband Ken have raised a beautiful Christian family.

JUST IN TIME

She was larger than life, the kind of person who knew no stranger, whose smile always lit up the room, and who always found the good in every situation. I met Kenon at Westmont College in 1984. I was her Resident Assistant; she became my soul friend and my bridesmaid. The day before my wedding, she showed me a lump under her collar bone. By the time I returned from my honeymoon, she had already begun chemotherapy. She battled cancer for 28 years. Cancer never stole her joy or her mission to do good while she walked this earth; in fact, it was the joy of the Lord that was her strength. Her love for Jesus grew deeper and faster than the cancer.

Kenon's faith was a canvas for all to witness the glory of our great God.

There are times in life when something unusual happens, and coincidence is not sufficient to explain it. In the summer of 2014, six days before she died, I had a rare glimpse of the eternity God had placed in Kenon's heart. It was a lazy July day, and I was reading *The Hiding Place* by Corrie Ten Boom to my son Broder. I read a passage that so gripped me that I immediately grabbed a highlighter and said, "I need to text this to Kenon." I felt a sense of urgency because I knew Kenon's days on earth were few. I picked up my phone and wrote, "I am reading *The Hiding Place*. God is so big. I have a passage I want to share with you." Kenon's response was immediate, "YES, FAVORITE BOOK." She continued, " My very favorite part of the book is where Corrie is afraid that her father will die. Her father deals with Corrie's fear by saying, "Corrie, when you and I go to Amsterdam - when do I give you your ticket?"

"Why, just before we get on the plane," said Corrie. "Exactly, and our wise Father in Heaven knows when we are going to need things, too. Don't run ahead of him, Corrie. When the time comes that some of us will have to die, you will look into your heart and find the strength you need — just in time."

Then Kenon texted, "what part of the book did you like?" I texted, "That was it! I kind of have chills right now. Just like I said-God is big!" It was the last text we shared. It came just in time.

We cannot fathom what God has done and will do from beginning to end; but in those rare moments, He allows us glimpses.

In memory of the beautiful life of Kenon Ramsey Neal

12/8/1965 - 7/16/2014

Katherine's verse: So is my word that goes out from my mouth: it will not return to me empty, but will accomplish what I desire and achieve the purpose for which I sent it. (Isaiah 55:11)

My verse for Katherine: Praise be to the God and Father of our Lord Jesus Christ, the Father of compassion and the God of all comfort, who comforts us in all our troubles, so that we can comfort those in any trouble with the comfort we ourselves have received from God. (2Cor 1:3-4)

Vincent DeSalvo, Writer/Producer/Director/Lifelong friend, Irvine, CA

Vince is incredibly smart and creative, truly a fascinating person. My husband Joe and I have been friends with Vince and his wife Randal forever, and have taken some memorable trips with them. We may not see them very often, but when we meet again, we can immediately pick up that sincere friendship effortlessly.

THE EPIPHANY

I suppose it's fair to say I'm more fortunate than most people, but more about that later.

The early 90's were the "Tale of Two Cities" period of my life. You know, best of times – worst of times. My business was flourishing. The years of hard work, sacrifice, and loss of family time were paying off at last. But it doesn't take a physicist to remind us that every action has an equal, yet opposite reaction. So while my professional life was on the upswing, my personal life was crumbling under its own weight.

My wife and I separated. We were both unhappy in our marriage and needed a break from each other. I bought a townhouse a few miles away from our home, where my wife continued to live. We remained close in proximity, but emotionally, we were at opposite ends of the earth.

And thus began possibly the worst period of my life. I was rudderless, living my life in concentric circles, unhappy, miserable, and sometimes violent. Something was missing, but I couldn't figure out what.

I was raised a Roman Catholic in an Italian-Catholic family. I even flirted with the priesthood for a time and spent a year in the seminary. But now, like so many Catholics, I became lapsed. I stopped attending Sunday Mass. In fact by then it had probably been several years since I attended Mass on a regular basis.

I still believed in the existence of God, but I was so unhappy I just couldn't see the point of practicing my faith any longer. After all, what had God done for me lately?

The unhappiness was followed by clinical depression. I would suddenly burst into tears for no apparent reason. I cried at work. I cried in the middle of a tennis match. I cried in front of perfect strangers. I was out of control.

Late one night, unable to sleep, I sat on a bluff overlooking the Pacific Ocean at Laguna Beach. I stared out into the darkness and once again began to cry. I was coming apart. My tears turned to screams as I yelled at God to give me the answer, lift the darkness from my life, and end my suffering.

At that instant, I felt a shudder course through my body. It wasn't imagined; it was real, and it was palpable. My body literally shook. Was the hand of God touching me, or was my mind playing tricks?

And then I realized the Father was simply trying to get my attention. You see, He had a message for me, and He wanted to make sure I was listening. The message was short and simple, yet so incredibly profound.

That's it. That is all there was to it, and that was all I needed. His message was crystal clear. No further explanation necessary.

The following Sunday my butt was in the pew at Mass. Then I started attending daily Mass and soon the darkness was lifted. It has been over twenty years since that night in Laguna and I have not had a single dark day since.

My wife and I fixed our broken marriage, and it is stronger than ever. We will soon celebrate our 40th wedding anniversary.

Which brings us back to where I began: I boasted I was more fortunate than most people. Let me explain.

Even those of us who believe in the existence of God, from time-to-time, have a moment of doubt. Yet we continue to believe. That's called Faith. We continue to believe even though at times, that Faith is shaken.

But on that darkest of nights in Laguna Beach, God revealed himself to me. I no longer have to wonder. I no longer have those moments of doubt. He spoke directly to me. He let me look behind the curtain and said, "Here I am. I'm real. I exist.

How can I help?"

And so he did.

My verse for Vince: Faith is being sure of what we hope for and certain of what we do not see. (Hebrews 11:1)

Don Waddell, Retired Minister, Southeast Christian Church, Louisville, KY

Don was an Air Force Colonel and flew combat missions in Vietnam, and later worked at the Pentagon. He is extremely competent and held pivotal ministerial positions in his church. He is tried and true, a Christian who puts his beliefs in action.

GIVING THANKS IN ALL CIRCUMSTANCES

I remember when I first heard the words "Multiple Sclerosis" and knew they were going to affect me personally. The words sounded hideous and ominous. At the time, I was a 23-year-old Air Force 2nd Lieutenant, and Nancy and I were stationed in Ohio. She was pregnant with our first child, and we had returned home to visit our parents. While at home Nancy's mother suggested she visit her family doctor. She complied, and I drove her to her appointment, remaining in the waiting room until summoned for a private conversation.

Her doctor explained that Nancy had had some abnormal neurological symptoms when she was 19, and he thought she might have MS. Nancy was unaware of this diagnosis, but her doctor wanted me to know in case there were complications with the pregnancy. I cannot adequately express my feelings following my meeting with Nancy's doctor. I had visions of wheel chairs, canes, and nursing homes. It didn't seem fair. We were so young and just beginning our lives together and looking forward to starting a family. "Why, God? Why are You allowing this to happen to us?" I wondered to myself.

When I learned Nancy might have MS, I had to consult a medical dictionary for details. I learned that Multiple Sclerosis is a chronic, often disabling disease of the central nervous system. Symptoms may be mild such as numbness in the limbs or severe involving paralysis, loss of vision, and occasionally death. Most people with MS are diagnosed between the ages of 20 and 40, but the unpredictable physical and emotional effects are normally lifelong. Nationwide, there are an estimated 250,000 to 350,000 people with MS. There is no known cure, but Nancy took injections of a powerful drug every other day for 17 years, which seemed to suppress major exacerbations.

Shortly after I was told of Nancy's diagnosis there came a time to tell Nancy. The news was a surprise, but she accepted it, confident that God would take care of her. Still, given the nature of the disease, a definitive diagnosis was elusive in 1968. One of the frustrations was that she appeared normal to others, even some doctors. For years afterward, Nancy had recurring periods of extreme fatigue, blurred vision, numbness in left side, and some occasional motor problems. Every 6-8 years she had a major exacerbation which left her essentially bed ridden for one to three months. It was during one of these exacerbations in 1988 that we finally got a definitive diagnosis due to the development of the MRI.

At the time of her attack then, we were in the process of moving from Soesterberg, Holland, to Bitburg, Germany. I thank God for our Air Force family who helped us to relocate. At one time I had two kids in Holland, one with me in Bitburg, Germany, and Nancy in a hospital in Ramstein, Germany. The moving van was somewhere in between. But we got the job done, and Nancy eventually got back on her feet.

Nancy was always getting the job done despite her illness. She seldom complained and never asked "why me?" She raised three kids despite her disease and the rigors of 22 moves in 28 years. She was the perfect, though sometimes absent, Air Force officer's wife often going to obligatory functions when she didn't feel like it because she knew a spouse's support socially was often a factor in an officer's advancement and promotion.

I recall one heroic episode in particular. In September, 1978, I had left Virginia for Holland, and Nancy and the kids were to join me as soon as I could find housing. For three weeks I searched for housing, met new friends, flew jets, and had a pretty good time while Nancy closed on the house, took care of a million details associated with the move. Then she got on a plane with our three kids, ages 11, 9 and 7, and flew to Europe. Unfortunately, the weather in Holland was so bad their airplane could not land, and she had to spend 28 hours in London's Heathrow Airport lobby with three energetic kids. Later they flew to Brussels and were bused to Holland. When I met her in Amsterdam, she was exhausted and weak. I hated it that she felt so badly. I felt guilty that I had put her though all this because of the career I had chosen.

But our experience with MS was not without its lighter moments. When we were stationed in Maxwell Air Base in Alabama, I had an MS-like episode. On that particular morning, I headed off to work, riding my bike, which was my usual mode of transportation. I felt dizzy and fell off my bike several times before I got to work. This was pretty unusual, even for me. Nancy had to take me to the Air Force hospital to see a doctor who administered numerous neurological tests before sending me to a downtown hospital for an MRI.

It was seven in the morning the next day when I received a call from my Air Force doctor advising me to come and see him as soon as possible. Egad! That sounded serious, and my mind began imagining all the worst-case scenarios---an inoperable brain tumor, a stroke, or some other life threatening illness.

Nancy and I waited in the doctor's office for what seemed like an eternity and held hands awaiting the news. The doctor had a serious look on his face as he sat down with the MRI results, and peering over his reading glasses said, "Colonel Waddell, the results of your MRI suggest you have Multiple Sclerosis." He paused to let that sink in. Nancy and I looked at each other in disbelief and then started laughing. Actually, that wasn't the reaction my doctor was expecting following his diagnosis of a serious, life changing disease. "I didn't know it was spread that way!" I joked. After the laughter subsided, I explained that the reason we reacted the way we did was because Nancy had MS, and his announcement was so unexpected. Some months later, we learned from another doctor that I had had a little bitty stroke, which resolved itself, and I have had no other symptoms since then.

I am sharing the story of Nancy's and my experience with MS for a couple of reasons. One is to let you know that we have discovered the scriptural truth that we really can give thanks to God even in difficult circumstances. Nancy's illness has drawn us closer together, and we're grateful she has a relatively mild case of MS. We certainly have learned to appreciate the times when she feels normal. We also understand that God can use suffering to accomplish His purposes, to bring Him glory, and to spread the Gospel.

But I also write to tell you how proud I am of Nancy and what she's been able to accomplish though she is stricken with a chronic and debilitating disease for over a half of a century. She has used her illness to glorify God and share her faith. Over the years she has ministered to many newly diagnosed MS victims and organized an MS Support group at our local church. Best of all she's been a loyal wife for almost 50 years now, and we have learned to *"give thanks in all circumstances."*

Don's verse: Be joyful always; pray continually; give thanks in all circumstances, for this is God's will for you in Christ Jesus. (1 Thessalonians 5:16-18)

My verse for Don: In the same way, the Spirit helps us in our weakness. We do not know what we ought to pray for, but the Spirit himself intercedes for us with groans that words cannot express. (Romans 8:26-27)

Gail Wenos, God's child who happens to have been blessed with CSP and CPAE, National Speakers Assn., Kane'ohe, HI

Gail is a professional speaker and ventriloquist, and her side-kick is a clever little guy named Ezra. She and Ezra speak before audiences, and when there is time, they visit senior communities to encourage the elderly. They use music, humor, and audience participation with a result that the recipients become children again. Gail is a beautiful Christian; she walks her talk. She became the caregiver to Ruth her friend in Christ.

ON THE FRONT END

"See, I am doing a new thing! Now it springs up; do you not perceive it? I am making a way in the desert and streams in the wasteland." (Isaiah 43:19)

January, 2015. I was ready for something new. Years of caregiving had taken a toll on me in every area of my life. I was beyond weary. Every month, the women of my church would meet for a time of fellowship and teaching from our pastor's wife, Debbie Williamson. In spite of the effort it took to be able to attend, I looked forward to those "Grateful Gatherings"....to soak up the love, simply sit, and listen.

Little did I know that as I sat there on that January morning, God would use Debbie's teaching to powerfully impact my life. She began by saying that "Hind sight is 20/20." A crisis hits. We fret and stew...begging God for His help, but not really trusting in His Sovereignty. Once the crisis is over and our heads are a little clearer, we look back and find ourselves surprised to realize that God had been with us through it all. We say, "Oh! NOW I see how God was working on my behalf! Oh! NOW I see how He gave me the strength to get me through!"

And then Debbie challenged us by saying, "How much richer and deeper would the blessings be if we could *trust God on the front end*." I had no idea that over the next several months those six simple words would prove to be transformational for me. But, as I learned to trust Him on the front end, I would not only experience His presence in the moment, but would be blessed by His unfailing faithfulness in some truly miraculous ways...for example:

For the past 15 years, I have been the primary caregiver for my very dearest friend Ruth. After living under the same roof for 40 years, we were more like soulmate sisters....family for each other. Because we were two single women with no family of our own, we considered many of our friends as extended family. We were blessed to be the "Aunties" to many of our friends' children. What a joy to watch them grow through the years. But as Ruth's health began to decline, our active involvement became more limited.

As Ruth's needs grew, the caregiving demands on me also increased, and I was becoming exhausted. Some of our "family" in Hawaii was so concerned that they would come to us in California to care for Ruthie and give me a break. They encouraged us to consider moving to Hawaii so that Ruthie could be surrounded by loving family, and I would have ongoing help with the caregiving. It sounded like a good idea...we tried... twice. Our house actually sold in ONE day! God said "No." The buyers backed out 10 days later.

When it became obvious that Ruth was too ill to move, she began to see things differently. She said, "I know I WILL be moving, but it won't be to Hawaii. It will be to my new home in Heaven." And then she said, "As soon as I'm gone, I want you to put the house back on the market and move to *your* new home in Hawaii...you need to be with "family." She was insistent on that idea and made me promise that I would at least try once more. All I could think of was, "I really need to trust God on the front end here."

Ruthie did "move" to Heaven on October 13, 2015. Did I put the house on the market? No. I was too overwhelmed to even think about it. The saying, "Don't make any major decisions for at least a year after a loved one's death" truly made sense to me. The "move to Hawaii plan" was put on the back burner as my major focus became facing the grief and finding my "new normal." There was, however, one persistent thought that kept surfacing throughout the next several weeks..."Gail, if you are supposed to move to Hawaii, God will let you know. Rest in that and trust Him on the front end."

God let me rest for seven weeks. Then out of nowhere, I received a letter from a couple interested in buying a home in my development. My model was the only floor plan they wanted. They asked if they could come and see it on December 4. When I explained my situation and told them that I really didn't want to make any major moves until at least September, their response was, "No problem. We won't be ready to move until September either." ONLY God could make this happen!

To make a long story short, they came, they saw, they bought. The house went into escrow in December, closed in March, and I became their renter as of April 1... (At a blessed ridiculously low rent!) It was a seamless transaction and amazingly stress free! But God had another HUGE blessing in store for me. Because this was considered a private sale, there was NO commission!! What I would have paid in commission will instead pay my rent in Hawaii for an entire year!

And speaking of renting in Hawaii, although my home had sold, the next question was WHERE would I be renting? I had no specific address...but I KNEW God did, and He would reveal it in time. My job was to "trust Him on the front end."

I knew that I would be going to Hawaii for five days in July to be a part of a 50th Wedding Anniversary celebration. On my last day there, I made an appointment with a rental realtor to see what might be available in September. Everyone told me not to expect to find anything in one day..."it just doesn't work that way," they said. So, I went with no expectations. However, God brought to my mind the verses from Isaiah 55:8-9: "For my thoughts are not your thoughts, neither are your ways my ways," declares the Lord. As the heavens are higher than the earth, so are my ways higher than your ways and my thoughts than your thoughts." With those verses firmly planted in my heart, I heard myself saying, "Well, with the amazing way God has gone before me in these past few months, it wouldn't surprise me at all if He shows me my new home while I'm here."

To once again make a long story short, I went, I saw, I rented.... in ONE HOUR!! And, it was FAR above and beyond my expectations!... "Immeasurably MORE than all I had asked or imagined" (Ephesians 3:20) I had asked for 2 bedrooms; He gave me 3. I asked for a nice view; He gave me an unobstructed view of the ocean AND mountains. I asked for a place that would feel safe; He gave me my own enclosed garage and a 24/7 patrolled security. I asked for a place that would be a "safe haven"...a place of blessing and respite for those He sends to my door...He did just that!

My last day in the house that was home for Ruthie and me for the past 15 years was August 31. The preparations for moving have begun. The "dominoes" have fallen into place, and God's fingerprint is on each one. He truly IS doing a new thing, and yes, I DO see it! He has "made a way where there seemed to be no way!" I am beyond grateful and humbled by His faithfulness. And now, as I move into this new chapter of my life, I'm excited to see what He has in store for me. But even as I face the unknown, there is NO question in my mind that HE is already in that unknown. Trusting Him on the front end is the ONLY way for me to live.

Gail's verse: "For I know the plans I have for you," declares the LORD, "plans to prosper you and not to harm you, plans to give you hope and a future." (Jeremiah 29:11)

My verse for Gail: God is not unjust; he will not forget your work and the love you have shown him as you have helped his people and continue to help them. (Hebrews 6:10)

Brad DeVries, Regional President, HomeServices of America, Louisville, KY

Brad is a wonderful Christian man, and he and his wife Jennifer have 8 children. He was a Harrier pilot in the United States Marine Corps, flying 39 missions in the first Gulf War. He leads four regional real estate firms for HomeServices of America.

PROTECTED FOR A PURPOSE

Like many men, I am guilty of walking through life day by day, not noticing how one fits with the next, and leading to weeks, months, and years. I am also guilty of somehow believing that I am in control of that journey, not realizing the true reality of God's sovereignty. Proverbs 16:9 says it the best: "In his heart a man plans his course, but the LORD determines his steps."

As I reflect back on my life, I can see three very distinct acts of protection that the Lord provided, and one very defining mo-

ment of redirection... All of which ultimately led to a beautifully restored marriage, family, and life.

Having been in love with the effects that alcohol had on my
system and overall self-confidence, I chose to partake heavily
during a wedding reception for my college roommate and his
wife. In an act of selfishness and poor judgment, I chose to get
behind the wheel of my girlfriend's car and drive the back roads
of Kentucky all the way back to campus... probably an hour
drive in the wee hours of the night. Less than 3 miles from my
destination, I fell asleep at the wheel, careening off the road
and straight through a telephone pole. Severing the wooden
pole at its base, and with seatbelt unbuckled, my head plowed
straight through the windshield. At probably 45 mph, no one
should have survived that accident. I walked away with some
glass in the top of my head, and not as much as a headache.

In 1988, I was a pilot in the United States Marine Corps. While
on a weekend mission to an Air Force Base in Alabama, I was
attempting to land a single piloted aircraft called the AV 8B
"Harrier." Due to three different malfunctions at one time in
the airplane, I found myself at over 120 miles per hour heading
straight off the runway and into a gently sloped grassy area.
With everything I could muster, and relying on every technique
I had ever learned, I desperately tried to bring the airplane to a
safe stop. The last thing that I remember was a severe crushing
sensation, followed by a heavy thud. What I ultimately realized was that the airplane had begun to flip over on its back,
which had I stayed with it, would have not been survivable.
Instead, I apparently made a last-second decision to eject from
the airplane, however only enough to pull half of the ejection
handle out. I will save you all the details, only to tell you that

had I pulled the other side of the handle instead, the parachute would have never deployed. The side that I happened to pull was the side that activated the low altitude capabilities, opening the parachute immediately. I never remember deciding to pull the handle; I was supposed to pull the whole handle, and had I pulled the other side instead, I would have been dead. Again, I walked away with nothing but a few scratches.

During this period in the Marine Corps, Jennifer and I survived the worst five years I could ever imagine in a marriage. We both knew who the Lord was, but neither of us was following Him. It could not have been more volatile, or self-centered, or more void of a spiritual foundation. There was no God, no Jesus, and no hope.

We were at the brink of divorce, when thanks to a seldom experienced moment of passion, God allowed Jennifer to conceive our first child Olivia. While I would never recommend starting a family in the midst of marital crisis, her pregnancy was what God used to awaken both of us, and to redirect our lives back towards our Savior! It should also be noted that five years prior, we tried with no success to have children. We went through two surgical procedures for Jennifer, but to no avail. Once again… God's protection and His timing were perfect!

Today I see the results: our oldest daughter and her husband leading a Bible study filled with young Christian couples, many who are new believers; our oldest son a youth pastor at a small Church in South Florida; his twin sister joining her new husband in his new role as an FCA (Fellowship of Christian Athletes) chaplain for 30+ schools in the local area; and our third daughter actively ministering to broken young women and finding help and hope in a local pregnancy resource center… God's purpose has been perfectly clear. The bride of my youth, 32 years later, is constantly pursued for her Biblical wisdom by women of all ages and walks of life. Her love for the fatherless and for "the least of these" makes her the most beautiful woman I have ever known!

Had God allowed me to perish in the car accident, in the airplane accident, or had He allowed our marriage to dissolve when it was all but over… All of this would have been missed. I am ever so grateful for His protection, and that He chose to beautifully guide my steps in spite of the plans I had laid out for myself!

Brad's verse: For I was hungry and you gave me something to eat, I was thirsty and you gave me something to drink, I was a stranger and you invited me in, I needed clothes and you clothed me, I was sick and you looked after me, I was in prison and you came to visit me…the king will reply, I tell you the truth, whatever you did for one of the least of these brothers of mine, you did for me. (Matthew 25:35-36, 40)

My verse for Brad: The LORD will guide you always; he will satisfy your needs in a sun-scorched land and will strengthen your frame. You will be like a well-watered garden, like a spring whose waters never fail. (Isaiah 58:11)

Amos Martin, Former Pro Football Player, Home Builder, Speaker, Author, Louisville, KY

Amos is a former NFL linebacker for the Seattle Seahawks. Locally, he is a very respected home builder with a reputation of honesty and integrity.

ONE SWIPE OF HIS FINGER

My wife and I love to hike and experience the beauty of God's magnificent creation. Our hiking expeditions started several years ago in Sequoia National Forest and Yosemite National Park. Seeing the largest trees in the world as well as the rock formations, lakes, and waterfalls of Yosemite was the highlight of our hiking involvement until we went to see the Grand Canyon.

We arrived at the visitors' station and discussed different options with the park ranger, and then we meandered to a location where we would see the Grand Canyon for the first time. As we walked through the partially wooded path to one of the viewing stations, I had no idea what I was about to see. Through the clearing and there it was…I stopped in my tracks, my jaw dropped, and I gasped for air. My first thought was, "God has been here. This could not be real!!!"

Everyone has viewed pictures, watched documentaries or films of the Grand Canyon, but nothing compares to being there. The Grand Canyon is simply unbelievable, and all the descriptive adjectives cannot help you perceive the magnitude of this amazing wonder of the world. There is nothing comparable in all the world, so how could there be any explanation other than a mighty and awesome God designed this one-of-a-kind spectacle?

In the beginning, God created the heavens and the earth. (Genesis 1:1)

The secular world may attempt to explain this massive gorge with theories about thousands of years of erosion, but I know God carved this spectacular canyon with one swipe of His finger. Maybe He sat on the rim and doused His toes in the river, but this is His masterful work. We could feel His presence as we viewed this remarkable creation, and our hearts pounded because we knew He and His mighty Holy Spirit dwells within our very souls.

Amos' verse: We know that we live in him and he in us, because he has given us of his Spirit. (1John 4:13)

My verse for Amos: For you make me glad by your deeds, O LORD; I sing for joy at the works of your hands. (Psalm 92:4)

Louise "Nena" Yokum, Retired Missionary, Navajo Indian Reservation at Burnt Corn, AZ, Normangee, TX

Nena is my sister-in-law who lives in Texas. She has had many difficult challenges in her life, and she says her faith has gotten her through them. Nena has a strong faith and I love to talk to her about Jesus. I am fascinated with her past life on a Navajo Reservation, and she has chosen a story about just that time in her life.

GOD IN THE MIST

I had a calling earlier in life as a missionary on the Navajo Indian Reservation in northeast Arizona. To live with the Navajo, one must learn their culture and accept their way of life. Every year was a new experience and presented new surprises in every way, but God led me there so I accepted His calling.

In July of my fourth year on the Reservation (REZ), we had planned to have a Vacation Bible School (VBS). I arranged to have my son from Mississippi and my daughter and grand-daughter from Houston travel to the REZ with a bus-load of church volunteers to help the Navajo and participate in the VBS.

Winter on the REZ is very cold with lots of snow, ice, and isolation. After such a winter, the Navajo and I looked forward to VBS with family and the anticipation of meeting new friends. In order to plan such an event, a year of preparation and coordination was necessary to arrange for the activities, as well as, the accommodations, food, and security for the incoming Bible Team.

About a week before the VBS event, disaster struck! All the Indians went silent and stopped talking to each other. They did not attend the regular church services and the Indian children did not attend the regular Sunday Bible School. Everyone stayed in their homes, kept silent, and did not converse with anyone, including me! I made attempts to identify the problem, but to no avail.

Well, here we were! The church group was enroute to Arizona in a chartered bus with 42 eager workers aboard and all their gear including supplies for the big event...a "Mississippi Fish Fry with all the trimmings!" My son Kevin was bringing 6 cases of frozen Mississippi farm-raised catfish with french-fries and hush-puppies! He also had the necessary food, snacks, and drinks to feed the volunteers for the duration of their visit.

To escape the pressure of this mounting problem, I decided to get in my car and drive to nearby Windslow, AZ. As I was driving back to the REZ, I started to cry. Tears were running down both my cheeks as I began talking to God. As we talked,

I said, "I give this all to Your will, as I know you will take care of this!" At that moment, a "peace" came over me, and I knew that God had control of the situation. All was going to be alright!

When Saturday came, the church group arrived, and the Navajos drove up with the little children eager for the big event. Everyone mingled, introduced themselves, and enjoyed a "Mississippi Fish Fry with all the trimmings!"

Yes, our God is awesome and comes to our aid when we "ask" for His help! We fed over 100 Navajos and 42 church volunteers and began a truly successful Vacation Bible School. We also repaired roofs, heard some wonderful preaching (my son) and conducted a successful Bible School for the beautiful Navajo children and adults.

God said, "ASK AND BELIEVE, I WILL ANSWER," and He did just that in Arizona!

Nena's verse: Be still, and know that I am God (Psalm 46:10)

My verse for Nena: And the peace of God, which transcends all understanding, will guard your hearts and your minds in Christ Jesus. (Philippians 4:7)

Margaret Walker, M.Ed., NBCT (ret.), Educator, Speaker, Chapin, SC

Margaret is a fabulous storyteller, as you will see in the following story. She is very attractive, and she has a precious Southern accent. She has had a fascinating life, and even at one point, she taught English to incarcerated teens, a truly tough job for a Southern lady. She is so much fun.

BLESSED ARE THE MEEK

Although I felt like an eagle lives within me, my family always treated me like a chicken. Even my father, a prominent minister in the state, whom I adored, told me that it would be better if I didn't open my mouth to speak. Despite my stubborn, tom-boyish, slightly passive-aggressive nature, I learned to keep my true feelings to myself, to keep the peace, and to make the most of whatever the situation. Of course, I nearly burst at the seams trying to do this, but I managed to develop a strong faith and a personality that was considered well-adjusted, even "great." Yes, as an over-achieving-people-pleaser, I made even Pollyanna proud!

The problem with the Pollyanna perspective is that those rose-colored glasses often distort reality and relationships. Such was the case in my marriage. He was gorgeous, intelligent, athletic, and I thought I had entered the fairy tale of "Happily Ever After." Somebody, wipe off those glasses, PLEASE!!! Somebody did.

While working part-time for a business forms company, I attended a Positive Thinking Rally. Attendance was mandatory, and I was less than enthusiastic about that "no work" day, as I could have spent that time with my three-year old daughter. I made certain that my employer noted my appearance at the rally, since I planned for my disappearance as soon as possible. However, the speakers were fascinating, with each presentation better than the last. The purpose of the business portion of the rally was to generate and improve sales, set higher goals, increase productivity, meet and exceed quotas, etc. Ty Boyd was the emcee and introduced the first speaker – Art Linkletter. I was spellbound and I could feel the eagle inside me stirring. The next speaker was Robert Schuller, then Zig Ziglar, and the eagle reared its head and was looking sharp. The speaker that made the most impact on me was a man whose name was not as familiar as the ones who had spoken before. His message was simple, clear, and hit home for me with a carefully orchestrated, moving presentation of a poem. Reflecting on the day on my way home, I thought of all those who were inspired to set new financial goals and who, no doubt, could hear "ka-ching" ringing in their ears for themselves and their employers. As for me...I could only hear the noise of wings as the eagle was about to take flight, and I felt spiritually empowered. I cemented a resolve to make life better for myself and my child. If my marriage survived, great. If not, we would be alright.

My marriage was a living example of the movie, <u>Sleeping with the Enemy</u>. (I hope you can remember back that far. It will save a lot of paper.) It was a dark, dark time. My role had to change if we were all going to come out of it alive and with our sanity. I continued my part-time employment while I went back to school to obtain a teaching certificate, so that I could get a full-time teaching position, a regular salary, and a schedule that would coincide as closely as possible with my daughter's when she started school.

Fast forward twenty years. Life had been difficult. I found it necessary to divorce my husband. My daughter graduated high school and left for college. I taught English at the local high school. Spare time was spent in extra-curricular activities sponsoring men's and women's tennis, three cheerleading squads, the Academic Team, sponsor for the senior class, and the social director for the faculty. Actively involved in my church, I was a loyal and faithful member of a Sunday school class, the sanctuary choir, president of UMW, my church "circle," and lots of committees. Yes, life was difficult, but also busy and happy.

You know how you think sometimes, "Is that all there is?" I never wanted to question God's authority or His plan, but I did wonder from time to time if He really intended for me to be single the rest of my life. I was lonely and on my own even in (maybe I should say, **especially** in) my married life, so I had decided that was my lot. The eagle would attempt to be content, to be an example to others, never settle for less, and never compromise her values.

In the meantime, my busy-yet-socially-boring life led me to embark on a blind date, a whirlwind romance, and into a marriage with a man I barely knew. WHAT??! I know. I know. But…upon reaching my late 40's (I mean, **really** late) and having long since traded in my rose-tinted glasses for bifocals, I knew a good thing when I saw it. Our first trip was to Alaska on a small cruise ship. Actually, the trip had been prearranged with Al, my husband, and his four best friends (two couples) long before I was ever in the picture. Happy coincidence?

Our relationships and life perspectives were interesting, as one couple had been married for almost 40 years, the other about 10, and ours as newly-weds. We agreed to meet at the end of each day on the top deck to discuss our various points of view on the day's events. (I was not kidding myself. I knew they were checking me out to see if I was good enough for their friend!)

In the process, they asked me how I came to be who I am. We spoke briefly about family background, but I couldn't neglect telling of my "positive thinking" experience. I gave a brief summary, so as not to bore them with too many details. My husband and his friends were all professional speakers, so they laughed, joked, and told their own tales of the perils and pitfalls of those programs—the highs and lows—the good and the bad (the inside scoop), and I was mesmerized.

It was at this point that Al's very best friend in the group, Robert, began explaining to me the difference between a celebrity and a non-celebrity speaker. He said that's why I could remember the names of the celebrities, but not the others. "The rest of us," he told me, "are in that other category. You don't remember our names, but we have what we call "signature stories" that you DO remember. For example, you might not remember my name, but I do a poem called "A Touch of the Master's Hand." He continued on and on, but my jaw dropped and tears streamed down my face as I realized that I was talking to the man who had changed my life. When I told them about my experience, I had not mentioned that the title of the poem I heard that day was "A Touch of the Master's Hand."

I tell you this story because of the importance of trusting God, His plan, His process, His timing. Robert and Al had a bond of love and friendship that went far beyond any blood relative. They never went a day without checking on each other, although they lived 500 miles and 3 states apart. They lived, breathed, and thought as one. God's plan is so much bigger than our own. At the time I heard Robert and his testimony of the "Master's Hand," Robert did not even know who Al was. It would be three more years before they would meet. But...I had to hear Robert. Robert had to meet Al. Al had to meet me. I had to go on a blind date, and it only took twenty years for me to see how the pieces of God's puzzle for my life would begin to fall into place.

The pieces keep falling...and just for the record, the eagle is soaring!

Margaret's verse: Blessed are the meek, for they will inherit the earth. (Matthew 5:5)

My verse for Margaret: Those who hope in the LORD will renew their strength. They will soar on wings like eagles; they will run and not grow weary, they will walk and not be faint. (Isaiah 40:31)

Elizabeth Hoagland, Author of the Christian book blog: Worship with Words

This clever lady has a Christian book blog called Worship with Words that is a must-read. She has a very loyal following, and every time I read her blogs, I go right out and buy the books that she recommends. She makes it fun and entertaining and always includes some of her personal experiences in the blog. She seems to know all the Christian authors personally!

WHEN GOD FINDS YOU IN THE OPRYLAND HOTEL...

Being a consummate planner, last-minute-invites generally do not fly with me. However, a long lunch with a mentor of mine birthed a last minute invite to go to Nashville, Tennessee for the weekend a few years ago.

As God would orchestrate, I was able to go. I joined seven other gals, most of who were on staff at Southeast Christian

Church. We were off and running to attend a Christian Women's Ministry Conference at the Opryland Hotel.

We met at Starbucks at eight o'clock sharp; early morning drives merit quantities of caffeine. Our leader, Lynn Reese, had quite the agenda in mind with numerous stops. Shopping bags began to accumulate in the back of our cars.

Round about five o'clock in the evening, we finally hit the Briley Parkway. My sweet husband John called to check on us. He was beyond stunned to discover what normally would have been a three-hour drive, took us *nine* hours. Hey, a girl's gotta do what a girl's gotta do.

The Opryland Hotel was bustling with people. Our conference alone had almost two thousand women in attendance. There were a couple other similar size conferences going on simultaneously, thus the "human terrarium," as Eric Metaxas dubbed the hotel, defined full.

All eight of us were thrilled to have the opportunity to hear from several excellent speakers: Priscilla Shirer and her mother, Lois Evans, along with Marita Littauer and her mother Florence were some of the first speakers. Stormie O'Martian spoke on the importance of prayer, and Cindy Lerae Cruse-Ratcliffe led us in worship. Kathy Troccoli also gave a mini-concert one night.

The emcee was a sight to behold. Dressed to the nines, she walked energetically across the stage, captivating us with fun facts about whomever she was introducing—most impressive. I'm convinced being an emcee is one of the toughest jobs, trying to grab and keep the audience's attention. She was also one of the speakers, receiving the very last time slot—no easy feat. Her name is Pamela Shaw.

We all took copious notes as the conference progressed all too quickly. Take-home value was wonderful. For a church the size of Southeast, we gained lots of ideas for events to offer to our women's ministry.

During one of the breaks, our little group was standing in the lobby area talking. Kathy Troccoli approached my buddy Gwen as she had spoken at our church a couple of times and remembered working with Gwen.

The beautiful emcee Pamela Shaw came up to me. She said, "Don't I know you from somewhere?" I was speechless. I looked to my left and right, certain she could not possibly be speaking to me.

"Don't I know you from somewhere?" she repeated.

Finally I said, "Are you talking to me?"

"Yes," she replied. "I just know I know you from somewhere."

We began working backward. She lives in Bowling Green. I live in Louisville. College? Now we were getting somewhere: We both attended the University of Kentucky. Sorority? We were both Kappa Alpha Thetas. At about the *same time!!*

Then, as if time stood still, God removed the scales from my eyes, ears, and heart. He showed us we were at the University of Kentucky, *at the same time, in the same sorority.* Indeed, I did remember her. She was Pamela Waldrop and was one of the UK cheerleaders.

Where we differed, I am sad to report, was in our faith. Pam was part of what we then called "the God Squad." I was not. The God Squad met weekly, doing Bible studies in the Theta house living room. I was busy sowing some wild oats, clueless to what a Bible study was. Sadly, many of us lost girls made fun of the God squad.

But God...oh, you knew that was coming....but God stopped me in my tracks, right there in the middle of the conference. Exhibiting grace, Pam didn't bring up those bad memories. Instead, as if God himself spoke these words, she poured out pure, utter, beautiful redemption: "Elizabeth! Don't you see? We're not only sorority sisters, now we're spiritual sisters!"

Like a river, tears began to flow. God rescued and redeemed lil' ole me, in a sea of thousands of women and other conference attendees, right smack dab in the middle of the Opryland Hotel.

An interesting twist to this story: While this last minute invitation worked into my calendar, one missing point nearly caused me to not go. My dear friend and mentor Jane, whose skirts I still cling to, was not able to go on this trip. She basically told me to buck up and be a big girl and go anyway. Had I not, I would have missed out on God's blessing. After meeting Pam and realizing that we had come full circle, I called Jane and said, "You were right! I know now why I am here at the women's conference!"

Keep your eyes open, you never know where God will find YOU! He delights in second chances! We give you all the praise and glory, Lord.

Elizabeth's verse: Even to your old age and gray hairs I am he, I am he who will sustain you. I have made you and I will carry you; I will sustain you and I will rescue you. (Isaiah 46:4)

My verse for Elizabeth: Don't let anyone look down on you because you are young, but set an example for the believers in speech, in life, in love, in faith, and in purity. (1 Tim 4:12)

Phyllis Null, Urban Ministry Missionary, Cincinnati, Ohio

This lady is so selfless, committing her heart to God every waking minute of her day. She worked with ladies in the inner city to get their GED certification. She is happy, helpful, and humorous in work and in play. She has a firm grasp of the gospel and shares it easily and frequently.

Healer, Savior, and Friend

Our family was blessed with four children. Our son Justin, who was our third child, was born happy and healthy in 1981. He was a joy as a baby and a delightful toddler. When he was about three years of age, he began having night terrors that became more frequent the older he got. He was seeing and hearing things that just were not there, but we hoped that he would soon outgrow them.

Since Justin was born in the late fall, we decided to have him start kindergarten the fall after his fifth birthday. We hoped this decision would prove to help him mature a bit more. His kindergarten teacher was a seasoned educator, having taught over 25 years. Kind and conscientious, she was encouraging at parent/teacher conferences saying that Justin was well-behaved and a delight to have in her class. By the end of his kindergarten year, however, she recommended that he be placed in the K+ program rather than first grade because he displayed an excessive amount of "daydreaming." She felt the extra year of preparation would help him outgrow this inattentiveness and help him be more focused for first grade.

With his kindergarten year behind him, we were looking forward to a fun-filled summer. Within a week of school ending, we were at our local community pool enjoying fun in the sun, and I began to notice some abnormal behavior from Justin. I called him over to the side of the pool, and he didn't respond; he just kept walking away from me and staring off into space. It was obvious that he did not hear my voice. As I continued to watch him, he would display this behavior off and on while playing in the water. Within a very few minutes, I realized that he was having seizures, not grand mal seizures, but the kind of seizure that looked as if he was daydreaming and not paying attention to what was going on around him, the same behavior his kindergarten teacher had described to us. So Justin had not been daydreaming in kindergarten; he had been having petit mal seizures his entire kindergarten year.

I had diagnosed Justin just through watching his behavior because I was the only child in my family of four children that did not have seizures as a preschooler. I recognized the signs, symptoms, and behaviors that come with seizure activity. I felt both relief and anxiety with this discovery because I knew that our lives were about to change, but I did not realize how much and for how long. I began researching pediatric neurologists and made an appointment to take him for an evaluation.

Thankfully, we were living in Cincinnati, Ohio, at the time and were blessed to be very close to one of the leading pediatric hospitals in the nation. The doctor we saw had been in practice for over 40 years, and he was entertaining, kind, and compassionate. He even asked if my parents could come in and talk with him about my siblings and their seizure activity as children. We immediately fell in love with this doctor, who was a gift from God, as we didn't realize how much time we would soon be spending with him at Children's Hospital, doing blood work, testing, procedures, and more. The weeks turned into months, and the months into years.

The doctor confirmed my suspicions that Justin did indeed have epilepsy or some form of seizure disorder and that it had a genetic connection. So, here I was, the only one of four children that did not have seizures, with a child who had seizures. Justin was put on medication with the intention of controlling the seizure activity so it would not become a disruption to either our son's life or that of our entire family.

As Justin started back to school in the fall, the seizure activity increased. He went from having petit mal seizures several times a day, to complex partial, and then on to grand mal. Just about the time we thought he was adjusting to a medication, the seizure activity would change or increase, which would necessitate a change in medication. As meds were added to his regime, we saw his sweet, funny personality change. He became mechanical and flat emotionally. I often asked myself if the meds were worth these personality changes, but didn't know what else could be done.

By his second grade year, Justin was having around 100 seizures per day; all types and all unpredictable. He was floundering educationally; he could not retain what he was learning, and the constant interruptions of seizures caused him to have learning gaps conceptually. I educated both his teachers and classmates every year so they would know what to do and how to respond to his seizures. The students actually did better in seizure management than did the teachers and faculty. To the students this was my Justin's normal day activity, but to the teachers, it was an emotional disruption to their classroom as well as their own hearts. To say that Justin was well loved by all who knew him, might be an understatement!

We were finally able to get an Individual Educational Plan (IEP) written to accommodate his learning disabilities that were a result of the seizures. The Lord provided a wonderful special education teacher, fresh out of college, who within six months had Justin back on grade level. We continued to change and add medications, have more blood work and testing, and began attending a seizure support group for families, because all of this changed the entire dynamics of our family life.

By the time Justin was eleven, he was taking four different medications three times per day. He had taken 18 different medications for almost six years. Suffice it to say that our life was very stressful, and our pastor, church family, friends, and relatives continued to pray for his healing. We prayed and prayed; we waited and waited. After much prayer and no healing, our pastor asked if there was any sin we could identify in our lives that might be standing in the way of God's hand of healing. As we examined our lives, we did identify one area which we had been neglecting, that of faithfulness in tithing.

We confessed our lack of giving and asked for a new heart and a new direction for faithfulness in this area.

One Sunday our pastor and church elders asked if they could pray over Justin and anoint him with oil, the prayer of healing mentioned in the book of James. As a family, we gathered with them after the Sunday morning church service and prayed over him. In a little over a week, the seizure activity completely stopped. Soon after that, Justin announced to the doctor that he had been healed, and he had stopped all of his medications. The doctor told him that he could not just stop the medications so abruptly, to which our son said, "Either God healed me, or He didn't, and I choose to believe He did, so I am done with the meds." From that moment on, there was not one more seizure in his life! Did God heal Justin because we repented of our sin? Did God heal him because of the prayers of our pastor and elders? Or did God heal him because He loves him infinitely more than we ever could, and He decided to extend His mercy toward him after all these years of struggle? We don't know why, we just know He did!

Just for an update on our Justin...he never had another seizure! He is married with three beautiful children, and he is a Lieutenant firefighter/paramedic. All of the many hours which he spent at the hospital around medical professionals lit a passion and desire in him to help others in need. God has shown Himself as a Healer, Savior, and Friend throughout our lives. Our walk of faith has been challenged and changed all because of God's grace!

Phyllis' verse: Surely goodness and love will follow me all the days of my life, and I will dwell in the house of the LORD forever. (Psalm 23:6)

My verse for Phyllis: Consider it pure joy, my brothers, whenever you face trials of many kinds, because you know that the testing of your faith develops perseverance. (James 1:2-3)

Norb Hancock, Prison Ministry, Author of Sentenced to Serve, Louisville, KY

Norb made a mistake and paid dearly for it. God humbled him and transformed him into a servant of Jesus. Norb spends much of his time with prisoners who are looking to change their lives. Norb tells them about his own experiences and where they led him.

SENTENCED TO SERVE

I have had plenty of time to go over and over what led to prison. There was not one time I consciously did the wrong thing, but looking back, I walked in gray areas that I should have shunned.

In the banking world, I worked in a risk business. It always involved risk. I was known for my savvy in the buying and selling credit card merchant accounts. Sometimes I walked in gray areas, not illegal but not entirely right either. I knew there were potential problems, but the bank knew that as well. I allowed money and success to override good judgment.

I should have asked more questions and used more due diligence. I thought I was careful and deliberate, making sure that two other bank officers signed off on all accounts, but in the end it didn't matter. After just three months at the bank, I realized that many transactions landed in the gray area between right and wrong. When they seemed more wrong than right, I resigned. But those three months were costly. I should have walked away sooner. None of it had to happen.

When I talk with young men and women in the business world, I caution them that when you're doing business, if your heart and intellect tell you there is a problem, go with that. In your personal life or business life never measure right and wrong by the world's standards. Walk away no matter how much money it will generate or how many rungs you'll climb on the corporate ladder. Never ever think you are smart enough and lucky enough to get by.

The Bible says that Satan prowls like a roaring lion, seeking who he will devour. I was his prey. There are pitfalls and traps everywhere. Never let money, worldly needs, prestige, and honor override good judgment.

Listen to God. Even though I was a Christian, I let my ego and desire for fame and fortune override good judgment. Ultimately that led to prison and the end of my career. If it looks gray, stay away.

God had been absent in my life for many years. Even though I accepted Him into my life when I was 13 years old, as I grew older, I forgot the things that I had learned. I went my own way and left God behind.

In prison, I had to learn all over that God is my Provider. For the first time in my life, I had to depend on Him for my safety, for the food I ate, for favor with officers in the prison and with other prisoners.

When I renewed my personal relationship with Jesus, I began to go to the prison chapel to read and pray and get ready for Bible Study. I began walking four miles a day in the yard, talking to the Lord all the way. The first mile, I prayed for other people as I walked. The second mile, I prayed for favor, the third mile, I sang songs of praise to God, and the fourth mile, I just had fellowship with God. I used it to pray for my wife Diane, my children and grandchildren. I prayed for all my friends at home including my accusers. I just had fellowship. I found that I looked forward to this time every day. My faith became stronger.

I began to really know Jesus as my Lord and Savior. I began to talk to him as if he is my best friend, the best friend in the world. I spoke with him when there was no one to talk to, in the morning and at night. He loves me so much that he gave his life for me.

I have been home almost 15 years. It has not always been easy. I can say that I have been blessed, using what I learned in prison to help other brothers and sisters who are going into prison, those in prison, and those getting out.

I wished that I had used better judgment, surrounded myself with better friends and co-workers. I wish I had been a better father and husband.

It took prison for God to get my complete attention, and when I listened, He gave me back my life. I jumped into His arms and will be there for eternity. It is not too late for you to take that leap into His arms!

Do it now!

Norb's verse: Blessed is the man who does not walk in the counsel of the wicked or stand in the way of sinners or sit in the seat of mockers. But his delight is in the law of the LORD, and on his law he meditates day and night. He is like a tree planted by streams of water, which yields its fruit in season and whose leaf does not wither. Whatever he does prospers. Not so the wicked! They are like chaff that the wind blows away. Therefore the wicked will not stand in the judgment, nor sinners in the assembly of the righteous. For the LORD watches over the way of the righteous, but the way of the wicked will perish. (Psalm 1:2-6)

My verse for Norb: Create in me a pure heart, O God, and renew a steadfast spirit within me. (Psalm 51:10)

Doris Amis Foster, Homemaker, Precept Bible Teacher for well over 20 years, Louisville, KY

Doris is a beautiful lady who is never without a smile and a kind word. She is the person you want to be when you grow up. She and her husband John were married 61 years, a godly marriage and truly soul mates.

DIVINE ORCHESTRATION

B ack in the 1980's computers were being added to my husband's business, and because of this, territories were being consolidated. My husband's territory encompassed parts of four states. It looked like a square on a map. With computers three territories became one, and the expansion would require us to move from Louisville, Kentucky to Atlanta, Georgia. This was devastating to us as we were both very involved in our church. I was leading Precept Bible Studies, and he was an elder involved in a large building program.

We prayed and prayed for God to intervene, but to no avail. We felt he was too young to retire, and our hearts were torn.

Nevertheless, we put our farm on the market, and he went to Atlanta while I stayed home to prepare the house for sale. He flew out from Louisville early every Monday morning and would return to Louisville late on Friday night.

One person showed interest and visited our farm several times, but we received no offer. The company did not buy farms, only houses, so after a period of seven months of this lifestyle, we were becoming exasperated. We had our home Bible study group praying weekly, and the real estate people kept sending out information on our farm. We looked for houses in Atlanta that would incorporate both land and house in our new property to protect losing a lot in taxes, and we finally found a house that was beautiful but was much too large for the two of us as our family was grown.

After we had three appraisals within $10,000 of each other, the company told us they would make an offer on our farm. The appraisals weren't even close. Then they told us they would give us a bid. We called our prayer group together, and without telling them the amount, we put inside an envelope the amount we would take for our farm. We told them that if the company came up with that amount or above, we would believe it is God's will for us to move. However, if the company came back with less, we would have to find something else to do because we would be staying in Louisville.

When the company came back with 97% of what we had written down, my husband threw his arms in the air and shouted, "We don't serve a 97% God; we are not going anywhere!"

Now I will tell you the rest of the story for this is truly a God story, and now I am 84 years old and have seen the result of that decision.

My husband told the company to put him in sales out of our house, and we would be content. Instead, they put him on special assignment for three years, opened his office up again, hired his secretary back, and he had the most fun of his career, even going to Australia and all along he was able to work at the church. I was able to lead my Bible study classes and be near my brother when he died.

The one person who had looked at our property several times had bought land all around our farm and was waiting for us to become desperate to sell, so in reality, it had been sold all along. We had put a bid on the big house in Atlanta that was to be delivered at 10AM one morning, and as luck would have it, someone bought it the night before, and we did not have to go through with that sale.

But, again, that is not all the story.

I was able to continue to lead Precept Bible studies for many more years, and John served several terms as chairman of the church board of elders, and they led in the construction of the present campus of Southeast Christian Church in Louisville, KY. The church grew so rapidly that in his retirement he was able to step in for two years as a volunteer administrator until they could hire one. His early retirement gave him 27 full years to serve the Lord in many capacities at Southeast, and God keeps sending people my way to encourage.

Through the years our land has become much more valuable with a subdivision, new road, and big industry nearby. I continue to live on the land we dedicated to the Lord's use. When we bought the property almost 40 years ago, we built a pile of stones to indicate the significance of that spot, and a sign says, "When your children ask why these stones? Tell them the LORD has helped us. Fear Him forever."

This Easter was my husband's first one to be in the very presence of the LORD. While he worshipped our God in heaven, I and my family, worshipped with him at Southeast along with 37,890 people who attended the multiple services of our church with its four satellite campuses. Of course, my husband did not do this alone, but through him, our 100% awesome God who orders our ways and our days to complete the good work He began in us, has shown Himself to be Almighty and has a plan for each of us to bring others to Jesus! I see now how He orchestrated our staying in Louisville to be available to Him for His purpose. I see the rewards of our following Him. We have been humbled to have been used of Him and "He (certainly) has done all things beautiful in His time." We have truly lived the abundant life! Thank you, God. To God be the glory.

Doris's verse: "Let not the wise man boast of his wisdom, or the strong man boast of his strength, or the rich man boast of his riches, but let him who boasts boast about this: that he understands and knows me, that I am the LORD, who exercises kindness, justice and righteousness on earth, for in these I delight," declares the LORD. (Jeremiah 9:23-24)

My verse for Doris: ...the LORD's unfailing love surrounds the man who trusts in him. (Psalm 32:10)

Aletha Marcum, Retired Retail Chain Sales Manager for Random House Publishing, Louisville, KY

Aletha is my sweet neighbor, such a delight to be with. Joe and I went to a couples Bible Study in her home, and we have been friends ever since. Joe and I love to have dinner out with Aletha and her husband Steve. They are fun and interesting, and there is never a quiet moment. They are very open and sincere about their Christian beliefs.

GOD IS ABLE

From as far back as I can remember…I was taught about God and loving Jesus. My Father was a pastor, and my Mother was a faithful praying minister's wife. As a teenager, I wanted to follow in the teaching of baptism, and my father baptized me in the Green River. I taught elementary school children's church….read my Bible and tried so hard to understand how to keep from sinning….because that is what the legalistic church I was raised in taught. Of course this was an expectation I could not live up to. Unfortunately, I began slowly leaving my church and its teachings and sinking deeper and deeper into a sinful way of life. I was a prodigal daughter.

The funny thing about sin is that little by little it gets easier and eventually we become slaves to sin. Throughout my twenties and early thirties, my life became all about me. As I traveled around the country for my company...I know that there were many times when my life has been in imminent danger. I also know that the Holy Spirit, along with my mother's prayers, interceded and I was not harmed.

During this time...I had a very successful career and a lovely home and family...yes, there were problems, but for the most part, I felt I was dependent on no one and life was pretty good. All the time, I had the nagging feeling that something was missing...a big hole in my heart that the pleasures of life did not fill. One thing I know for certain...God is a patient and faithful God! During a business trip driving to Dayton, I listened to a sermon about being restored to God. Then and there I began praying for forgiveness and restoration. I called my parents and shared my experience with them.

I claimed these verses from Psalm 71:2, 17, and 20

Verse 2: Rescue me and deliver me in your righteousness; turn your ear to me and save me.

Verse 17: Since my youth , O God, you taught me, and to this day I declare your marvelous deeds.

Verse 20: Though you have made me see troubles, many and bitter, you will restore my life again.

I know that my mother was very faithful in her prayers for me...never giving up. Prayer is the only answer...never give up! GOD IS ABLE....I have experienced Him returning a prodigal to the fold more than one time and that includes me. Thank you, Jesus.

Aletha's verse: May the words of my mouth and the meditation of my heart be pleasing in your sight, O LORD, my Rock and my Redeemer. (Psalm 19:14)

My verse for Aletha: Search me, O God, and know my heart; test me and know my anxious thoughts. See if there is any offensive way in me, and lead me in the way everlasting. (Psalm 139: 23-24)

Gary Montgomery, Author, Speaker, and Trainer, Prime Time Productions, Louisville, KY

Gary is a friend to everyone; his smile is infectious, and his sincerity is warm and real. He is a celebrity but does not realize it. His faith is strong, and his personal relationship with Jesus should be an envy of every Christian. Gary has taught religious education to eighth graders for well over twenty-five years.

BRING IT TO ME

There is something bigger than me. Unfortunately, it has taken a lot of years for me to discover this truth; and, again unfortunately, I attempted to keep my eighth grade attitude alive while God was working with me.

As a youth, my focus was on me. Gradually, I started to understand there were things bigger than me. First it was Mom and Dad, my church, teachers at school, of course Uncle Sam and the Air Force, bosses at jobs I held, careers with the city fire department and 30 years of television broadcasting, and marriage with my number one boss, Judy.

I didn't put God in that initial list because He wasn't there.

It took me awhile to understand that God is bigger than me. The formation started early in my Catholic faith with the sacraments, Catholic schools, Sunday Mass, along with my parents' instruction and teaching. That was the foundation that kept me in the faith, but grasping the reality of God and His unconditional love came later as I experienced God through my relationships.

Once I understood that God is bigger than me I began to try and get out of the way and allow Him to take over my life. I have to admit that it wasn't easy for me, yet I continued to work on this.

I am reminded of some years ago when I was fired from WHAS TV, a television station in Louisville. They hired a new News Director. He didn't like sports, he didn't like me or the way I did my sports show, so my contract was not renewed. I was fired.

My predicament allowed me to start my current speaking business, and I eventually ended up at another TV station WDRB-Fox 41, also in my hometown of Louisville. But along the way there were some challenging adventures I had to confront before I re-learned that God is bigger than me and that I need Him in my life.

During the time I was building my speaking business, my income was greatly reduced. Gone was the comfort of working for someone else and receiving a weekly paycheck.

Building a new business was very challenging. Judy and I did not have enough money to make the house payment one month. We were $500.00 short and had no idea how to come up with it. We were learning there is someone bigger than us, and we were going to have to go to Him. We prayed fervently.

One morning Judy was distraught; she was greatly concerned and challenged. While taking clothes out of the dryer in the basement, she fell to her knees and prayed because there seemed to be no way to find $500.00.

A couple of days later my godmother Marie Quilty called. We had not talked in years, a lot of years. I later learned she knew that I was fired from WHAS, but she did not mention it; instead we had a pleasant conversation. At the end of our time on the phone, Marie asked if she could send me a note. I said of course and thought little about the request.

A few days later her card arrived. Inside was a check: the amount was $500.00.

Judy and I re-learned that God is bigger than us, and He is greater than our problems.

He is stronger than doubt, and He is more powerful than fear. He is more significant than any issue I have. His message to me is, "Gary, bring it to Me. I am bigger than your discomfort, your challenges. Let Me be the one to come to in times of fear. Gary, give it to Me."

That message is so simple; I don't know why I continually want to take over. Perhaps it's pride. Maybe doubt. I guess I believe I can take care of everything. I really do get in my own way. The message is simple: Trust and obey.

Here is what God has taught me and continues to teach me:

God shows me that He is alive in this world. I see and experience God's love in people and circumstances. I received an email from a friend who agreed to write an endorsement for my book. He was complimentary about what he read and said this, "I sincerely enjoyed your book. It brought a glow that I experience whenever I encounter the Holy Spirit." He said that something I wrote caused him to feel the Holy Spirit! Imagine that! Something bigger than me was using me to bring the Good News alive on earth.

Folks, there is something greater than us: It's God. And, when we allow ourselves to get out of the way, some amazing things can happen.

Just think about it! I don't have to solve all the problems, or try to understand them. Just give them up to God. He is bigger than me, and He is in control. Just trust. And He has taught me that when He takes away the challenges, the doubt, fear, anxiety, discomfort, God replaces those burdens with His yoke, which is easy to carry.

His yoke rests gently around my neck and supplies me with faith, trust, hope, love, confidence, and peace. It is a blessing to experience the gifts and the unconditional Love of God. It's all freely given. His gifts cause us to stand in awe and wonder when we try to understand just how big our God is.

God is good, all the time!

Gary's verse: "For I know the plans I have for you," declares the LORD, "plans to prosper you and not to harm you, plans to give you hope and a future." (Jeremiah 29:11)

My verse for Gary: The prayer of a righteous man is powerful and effective. (James 5:16)

Joe Donaldson, Director of the Potters Wheel Ministry, Host of Hopewell House, Friend of God, Louisville, KY

Joe is an incredible Bible teacher, always giving fresh insight into Scripture and delivering it with humor. In his Potters Wheel Ministry, he partners with other ministries to aid in the spiritual development of their members. His Hopewell House is a retreat house where participants get away to connect with God.

WHEN GOD SNEAKS UP ON YOU

I had the awesome advantage of growing up in a family that not only believed in God but desired to serve Him. From my birth, I was in the church with my parents and older brothers. I heard good teaching and received much good advice on the Christian life and the nature of God. I never doubted God nor strayed from the church through the normally tumultuous teenage years. I was very comfortable being a God follower. I was very comfortable with God.

During my sophomore year at The University of Kentucky (1980), I was sitting in a Biochemistry class which was probably a little over my head academically. It was a class that pretty much everyone in the medical sciences needed to take. All I knew was that I was going to have to study very hard to get a decent grade to keep in good standing. It was a large lecture class taught by a professor whom I assumed I would never meet. In those days I avoided any interaction with professors – especially ones who intimidated me with their intellect. All I wanted to do was get through this class so I could move on.

I remember almost nothing from the class including the professor's name. I am not even sure what building we met in, but I do recall that I sat by myself most days. All I remember is that God revealed Himself to me in a new way in that lecture hall – through the Kreb's Cycle.

As I said before, I was comfortable with God. I never really doubted God's existence or His role as Creator of the universe, but I also never really allowed myself to be amazed by Him either. While some Christians felt that the sciences were antagonistic to God, I simply didn't see the conflict. In reality, God was meant for Sunday mornings and family while the sciences were for school and a future career. That was until God met me in the Kreb's Cycle.

To the best of my memory, biochemistry deals with the chemical processes and compounds which are essential to the life of an organism – like humans. To me, biochemistry was simply a subject filled with difficult to remember (and understand) chemical processes which I needed to know well enough to move on to hopefully easier classes.

One of those chemical processes is the Kreb's Cycle, a complex series of reactions used by all oxygen breathing organisms to produce energy through the oxidation of acetyl-CoA which is derived from carbohydrates, fats and proteins into carbon dioxide and energy. The cycle also provides precursors of certain amino acids and other essential chemical agents. That overly simplified definition can be made even more simple by saying it is how we breakdown our food to produce chemical energy which fuels every function of our body.

As my professor explained, it is what happens when you eat a cracker and it results in you being able to run and jump. Somehow, that illustration turned a light on for me. For the first time, I was truly amazed by creation. To see the incredibly complex and yet beautiful cycle which had to occur to fuel my individual cells which in turn somehow worked together to allow me to not only live but to run and jump was, to that point in my life, my greatest revelation. For the first time, I was utterly amazed by the complexity of creation and therefore the awesomeness of the Creator.

I sat in that lecture hall totally amazed, and it suddenly became the finest worship center I had ever entered. I set down my pencil, I quit trying to take notes, and I simply sat in His power and beauty. God had snuck up on me in a place where I least expected Him. He met me in a place where I had not really invited Him. He met me in His creation as described by His evangelist that was disguised as a biochemistry professor. He met me in the Kreb's Cycle. He woke me from my spiritual doldrums to say – "See, this is the kind of God I am!" If we could have ended class with an invitation hymn, I would have gone forward to recommit my life. Instantly, my safe and manageable vision of God had been shattered by Him giving me a glimpse of just how awesome He is.

It is my understanding that there has been quite a bit of further discovery of the intricacies of the Kreb's Cycle since my class 35 years ago. In other words, it is even greater and more complex than we understood before. That shouldn't surprise us. The more we learn about His creation, the more amazing the Creator becomes. Every now and then I eat a cracker and marvel at the thought that there are incredibly complex chemical processes going on inside of me which will result in me getting up to run and jump – or these days, just reaching over for another cracker.

Joe's verse: For this reason I kneel before the Father, from whom his whole family in heaven and on earth derives its name. I pray that out of his glorious riches he may strengthen you with power through his Spirit in your inner being, so that Christ may dwell in your hearts through faith. And I pray that you, being rooted and established in love, may have power, together with all the saints, to grasp how wide and long and high and deep is the love of Christ, and to know this love that surpasses knowledge—that you may be filled to the measure of all the fullness of God. (Ephesians 3:14-19)

My verse for Joe: This is what the LORD says—your Redeemer, who formed you in the womb: I am the LORD, who has made all things, who alone stretched out the heavens, who spread out the earth by myself (Isaiah 44:24)

Mary Jane Mapes, MA, CSP, Author, Professional Speaker, Executive Coach, Kalamazoo, MI

Mary Jane is an engaging speaker, very genuine, very credible. From a family of eleven, Mary Jane wanted to stand out, and that she did!! She is a leader with organizational skills; just give her a project and she completes it beyond expectations.

WHEN PUSH COMES TO LOVE

It was the first day of a two-day communication course. The instructor, who was standing in the front of the room, said to us, *"Access to power in communication comes from being willing to give something up."* I thought to myself, *"Yah, well, I know that. I understand what it means to surrender control to get control."* I felt smug listening to what seemed like the obvious. Then, it was as if she had heard me thinking. Looking directly at me, she repeated, *"Now, hear what I'm saying. Access to power in communication comes from being willing to give something up. Give up the need to control; give up the need to fix; give up the need to make people different; just give it up."*

We had to create lists of people from whom we felt separated. Almost no one appeared on my lists. My dad was the only person who appeared more than once.

Now before you get the wrong impression, it's important for you to know that I loved my dad. He was hardworking… painfully honest…and he always set high standards, not just for himself, but for my seven brothers, my sister and me. The problem was that we had always been like oil and water. I would be in the room with him for 5 minutes, it was okay…10 minutes, it was a strain…15 minutes, and I wanted to punch his lights out.

There was nothing wrong with my dad. It's just that I grew up watching TV when it idealized fathers. I watched Robert Young as Jim Anderson in Father Knows Best, Hugh Beaumont as Ward Cleaver in Leave it to Beaver, and Ozzie Nelson who played himself in the Ozzie and Harriet Show. These were fathers who listened to their children; my father lectured. These were fathers who praised their children. My father always said, "Mary Jane, any fool can compliment you. It takes somebody who cares about you to show you the error of your ways so that you might grow up to become somebody." I always thought there ought to be a little more balance.

The instructor then said, *"Sometime between now and tomorrow morning, I want you to make a phone call to the person who shows up most often on your lists and say something that will change the course of your relationship with that person."*

I didn't want to call my dad. After so many years, why would there be any reason to believe that our relationship could ever be any different.

A group of us from the class went out for dinner that night. When we came back to the hotel, I went to my room, stood in front of the mirror, and mustered up the courage to make the call. Looking into the mirror, I gave myself a pep talk. *"Look, you're gonna make that phone call. You paid your money and you promised yourself that you would do whatever they asked you to do so you could learn whatever it is you needed to learn. Now, make the call."*

I took my phone out of my pocket, and prayed my parents wouldn't be home. My heart pounded, and my hand shook as I dialed my parents' home in Green Valley, Arizona, all the while reminding myself to *"give up the need to make him different."* They were home. My dad answered.

"Hi, Dad," I charged in. *"I just called to tell you that I went out to dinner tonight with some people, and one of the women in the group said that she thought that the most important thing to a parent was to know that their children were happy. And it dawned on me that it was probably important to you, too. Then I realized that you were probably the only person in my whole life who didn't know how happy I am. So, I called to tell you that I am very, very happy. I have a husband I adore, and I know he adores me. And I have two children – you know who they are ... Lisa and Joey ... who I honestly believe will be unstoppable once they figure out what they want to do and how they're going to do it. And, Dad, it's important for you to know that I love my work. Every morning I get up, I say, 'Thank you, Lord, for letting me do my work.' So, Dad, I want you to know that I am very, very happy. And that's what I called to tell you."*

Pause. There was dead silence on the other end of the line. I figured if he wasn't going to talk, I was going to take advantage of it, so I kept right on a-going.

"And, Dad, you have never known how happy I am because whenever I've gone home to visit you, I've never been happy. I have never been happy because I get tired of you always telling me what I should do and how I should do it. And tonight as I thought about how tired I get of you telling me what I should do and how I should do it, it dawned on me for the very first time how much like you I am. Whenever you start talking, I stop listening because I want to do the talking. And then Dad, I think I got it. I finally figured out that your lecturing me all these years has been your way of trying to tell me that you love me, and I have never really heard you because I've never really listened. So what I really called to tell you, Dad, is that I know you love me, and I want you to know that I love you, too... and that's really what I really called to tell you."

Pause. Nothing. Silence. *"Daaad? Are you there?"*

"Yes," he sounded stunned. *"You're right, Mary Jane. You and I are a lot alike. And you're right that your mother and I love all you kids very much. And, you're also right that the only reason I have ever tried to tell you or your brothers or your sister anything is because...."*

And he was off and running, just like always. But you know what? He didn't talk nearly so long. And I think it's because for the first time in my life I was actually open to receiving the gift that was my father, instead of secretly wishing he was different. And for the first time in his life, he must have known that his oldest daughter had finally heard him.

But the most powerful thing about that call was that for the first time in my entire life, from Green Valley, Arizona to Kalamazoo, Michigan, over the telephone, I truly experienced my father's love for me. And in that very moment, I discovered what it really meant to surrender to gain access to the love of my father – a gift that I could no longer refuse to accept.

That experience changed both of us. From that time on, he never hung up the phone without telling me he loved me, something he had never done before. But it also changed me. For in that moment, I learned what it really meant to *honor my father*.

By giving up the need to "fix" my father, I gained access to a genuine loving relationship with him that I enjoyed until his death almost 10 years later. Not a day goes by that I am not grateful for that instructor who created an experience by which I learned the true meaning of *access to power in communication*. Simple; just not easy. As paradoxical as it seems, we only gain access to control when we're willing to give up control and do the thing our Heavenly Father calls us to do: to love Him and love others as ourselves. When we are obedient, He never fails to bless us with the love of others we desire.

William James, Father of American Psychology, once said that the deepest human craving is to be found acceptable. The Book of Proverbs, 19:22 [NIV] says it this way: *What a man desires is unfailing love, ...* When we set aside judgment, all desire to "fix" someone else, we open ourselves to receiving the gift of another. God's way gives us access.

God wants us to enjoy all the blessings He ever intended for us. He is the ultimate Provider of every good and wonderful gift. When we are willing and obedient, He cannot help but bless us as that is His promise.

Mary Jane's verse: If you are willing and obedient, you will eat the best from the land (Isaiah 1:19)

My verse for Mary Jane: The LORD disciplines those he loves, as a father the son he delights in. (Proverbs 3:12)

Mary Rivard, Retired Human Resources Manager, Stoll Keenon Ogden, Louisville, KY

Mary is a friend, and she is delightful, poised, and confident. Even though she writes about some missionary friends in the passage below, she and her husband Dan also have a strong interest in the small town in Panama, contributing time and money into the service of that region.

ABIDING LOVE

I want to share a few of the amazing experiences of two dedicated, mission-minded Christian friends, David and Lisa Carter. Over ten years ago, after returning to the US from the mission field in Africa, a dear friend offered them the opportunity to run his Bed and Breakfast in Panama. They were excited to undertake the enterprise, knowing this would allow them to support and encourage the church there. About eight years ago, my husband Dan met them while on a mission trip to Panama with Global Children's Educational Foundation.

Meanwhile, a young Panamanian man, Nico Fernandez, was searching for God. He had grown up in a ghetto, but was striving to find a better life. This eventually led him to move to the small town of El Valle' where there was a local crafts market where many Panamanian and Kuna Indian artists sold their wares. One day two missionaries came into Nico's crafts booth. When they saw he was reading a Bible, they asked if he understood what he read. He told them he was trying, but some things were difficult to understand, so the missionaries told him that God would send someone to help him. Before they left, they gave him a paper with the name and phone number of someone who was teaching the Bible and English through the Let's Talk Program in Panama City. He thought it would be great if he could improve both his English and learn about the Bible. The problem was that Panama City was over three hours away.

About two weeks later, two more missionaries came into Nico's booth. He asked if they were missionaries, and when the woman said, "Yes," he showed her the paper that the previous visitors had given him. Her face got all red, and he thought he had said something wrong in his broken English. She assured him he had not said anything wrong and asked how he had come into possession of the paper -- because there were about 300 people in the market that day and it was her contact information! He explained that the other missionaries had told him God would send someone to him, and it must be her! In 2010, Lisa and David began studying and worshiping with Nico and his family and one other family in El Valle'. Nico was the first person in his town to accept Christ and to be baptized, and then his family also obeyed the gospel. David and Lisa moved to El Valle' to work with that small, but growing, group of believers. During this same timeframe, God also led them to a remote rainforest village of the Embera Puru people to teach the gospel.

Several people from our church in Louisville, Kentucky, had met David and Lisa in Panama and recommended them to our Missions Ministry. We began supporting them with money and mission teams. The church in El Valle' had been growing while meeting in their rented home, when their landlord informed them he would not renew their lease. Then God opened another door just around the corner from their home: A facility, formerly run by nuns to give orphaned girls an opportunity to attend camp, came on the market. Although the purchase process was long and complicated, they were able to purchase the property, which is now known as El Valle' Iglesia de Cristo.

Nico said he loves how David and Lisa treat everyone; they are always helping the people and working very hard. As an example, he told of a trip to the home of a lady who had cancer, for whom they had been providing support and encouragement. She did not attend the church, but they wanted to let her know that Jesus is the one in control. David and Lisa also work in the schools, helping wherever there is a need.

Lisa said when they arrived in Panama, they had no idea they would meet a man in a town in the mountains who was searching for God, or that they would come to know and love the people of the Embera village where more than 20 people have come to accept Christ as their Savior. David and Lisa visit the Embera people once a month, journeying for hours by van and dugout canoe to reach them. There had not been a New Testament church in either the Embera village or El Valle'. Working with these two congregations has become their full time ministry and primary focus. Nico is now studying to become a minister and teaching English at a college. The church in El Valle' now has a congregation of 80 people. They worship and sing praises to God in three languages: Spanish, Kuna and English. The love I have witnessed among them and shared with them testifies to the greatness of God and His abiding love for his people everywhere.

Mary's verse: Now this is what the LORD says—he who created you, O Jacob, he who formed you, O Israel; fear not for I have redeemed you; I have summoned you by name; you are mine. When you pass through the waters, I will be with you; and when you pass through the rivers, they will not sweep over you. When you walk through the fire, you will not be burned; the flames will not set you ablaze. For I am the LORD your God, the Holy One of Israel, your Savior. (Isaiah 43:1-3)

My verse for Mary: In his heart a man plans his course, but the LORD determines his steps. (Proverbs 16:9)

Greg Allen, BA from Milligan College, MDIV from Southern Baptist Theological Seminary, Louisville, KY

Years ago when I heard Greg speak and sing as worship director at church, my first impression was that the light of Christ exuded from this humble servant. My first impression has not changed. Greg is a wonderful example of Christ's love for his fellow man. He is now pastor at the Crestwood campus of Southeast Christian Church.

OVERWHELMED!

When David realized how often the Heavenly Father thought of him, he couldn't help but write it down so the world would know. What David wrote has become what we know as Psalm 139. Part of that journal entry states, "…How precious to me are your thoughts, O God! How vast is the sum of them! Were I to count them, they would outnumber the grains of sand."

A friend counted 1,850 grains of sand to a one-eighth teaspoon measure, which equates to 710,400 to one full cup. Once you consider the thousands of miles of seashore, hundreds of thousands of square miles of desert, and add to it the sand on the ocean floor, you can quickly become overwhelmed at the task of counting the countless number grains of sand.

That's the point, overwhelmed. To think of how often the Creator, the Heavenly Father Himself, thinks of me leaves me breathless, speechless. That's the point David was trying to make that day in his journal. The same is true for you. If you trust in Jesus, you are a child of God, and you are on the mind of the Heavenly Father so often that the number of times has yet to be invented. Overwhelmed.

Greg's verse: Therefore, if anyone is in Christ, he is a new creation; the old has gone, the new has come! (2Corinthians 5:17)

My verse for Greg: "Ah, Sovereign LORD, you have made the heavens and the earth by your great power and outstretched arm. Nothing is too hard for you." (Jeremiah 32:17)

Bob Gibson, VP Partnering Organizations, Team Expansion, Louisville, KY (Missions to the unreached)

Bob has a solid business background and uses it today in furthering missions in the far reaches of the world. He is very organized and concise; he loves to analyze and to look more deeply into every facet of his life, and as you will see, even when he considers how BIG God is.

GIFTS TO SERVE HIM

I was praying the other day and mentioned a praise to God for all of my body systems. After finishing the prayer time, I thought, "I don't even remember how many systems there are, let alone name each one." I was supposed to remember these from my school days of health & hygiene classes.

A quick search revealed that I am walking around with ten unique and complex systems that are continuously functioning without my thinking about them. God has put into repetitive cycles, ten essential life sustaining processes that must function properly in order for me to have a normal physical body.

I have been blessed and have often taken for granted all of these amazing gifts that allow me to serve Him. Unfortunately, we are still often without words to explain why some of our brothers and sisters are born with disabilities and others, due to accidents or other reasons are going through life with some body systems that are not working at 100%.

That quick search reminded me that our BODY SYSTEMS are:

Skeletal: Have you considered lately what an extremely capable tool the hand is like being able to unscrew a jar lid? How about the arm and your ability to reach something or even to be able to twist it around to touch your back?

Muscular: There are many in the world who can run marathons. For those of us who are not equipped this way, God has still granted many of us with normal muscles that have functioned for many years.

Nervous: Have you considered recently your body's reaction to something not normal touching the skin of your arm? Without thinking and immediately, you jerk your arm away from the pain-causing item. What a unique electrical system we have and so fast to react.

Brain: Where do we start here? Consider the thing that makes man uniquely different from animals: we have a brain that can reason. Our decision making ability is unique to us. Why do we pollute this organ by drinking alcohol or using drugs that directly affect the brain and cause us to function like animals?

Cardiovascular: How long has it been since you thanked God for giving you a heart and blood circulating system with miles and miles of vessels? This complex system includes blood circulating and transporting nutrients, oxygen, carbon dioxide, hormones, and blood cells throughout the body.

Heart: Isn't it great that we don't have to tell our heart to beat 70 or 90 times per minute? Yes, and it continues to repair itself while it continuously labors away.

Lymphatic: This is a network of tissues and organs including the bone marrow, spleen, thymus, and lymph nodes that produce and store cells that fight infections and disease: another big praise to God.

Digestive: Wow, cycle after cycle for how many years? I was reading in God's Chosen Fast, and Arthur Wallis said: "Without a doubt there are ills that could be cured or better still prevented if fasting, coupled with reformed eating practices were practiced. Oblivious to this, man still continues to dig his grave with his knife and fork."

Endocrine: The endocrine system is the collection of glands that produce hormones that regulate metabolism, growth and development, tissue function, sexual function, reproduction, sleep, mood, among other things. Have you ever thought of discarding this one and try to operate on nine systems?

Respiratory: I went for 80 years without having to visit a Pulmonologist (Lung doctor). A medicine, given to me to cure an arthritis problem, had after-effects that caused me to lose half of my lung capacity.

Obviously, today I have just fond memories of normal lungs, and my respect for God's gift of normal lungs is immense.

Bob's verse: I know that you can do all things; no plan of yours can be thwarted. (Job 42:2)

My verse for Bob: I praise you because I am fearfully and wonderfully made; your works are wonderful, I know that full well. (Psalm 139:14)

Joe Bonura, IV, Blessed husband to Karen and father to Joey, Aubrey, and Katie. Honored to also be foster parents, and maybe more, to others.

He is my older son who has had great challenges in his life, and he always reacted to them with great strength. He and Karen raised three beautiful children who have grown up and have wonderful careers. Joe has always had great compassion for others, his greatest asset.

WHY ME?

Why me? This is a question asked by so many for just as many reasons. I have had a few near death experiences in my life that have always left me wondering "why me?" and when I say this, it's not because I'm wondering how such a thing could happen to me, but rather why was I spared?

Most recently when I was 42 in 2007, I started losing the mobility in my left foot. I work out a lot and thought I might have a pinched nerve in my lower back. I had never been to a chiropractor and decided this might be a good time to go. He did tests and said I had a pinched nerve in my lower back and with seven more treatments, it should be fine.

The next day while I was driving, my left arm dropped, and instead of turning left to see a customer, I made a right and drove myself to a hospital. They admitted me right away which was the first red flag since there was a waiting room full of people. The ER doctor did many of the same physical tests as the chiropractor the day before, but ordered me to go right in for a CT scan. The scan showed a golf-ball-sized tumor on the right front lobe of my brain.

All of my family was notified what was going on. My amazing wife Karen was on a field trip with my two daughters in Columbus, Ohio when she got word. She rented a car and would have beaten any jet back to Louisville. I know God was driving that day!

While she was on the way back to Louisville, I was on another table having an MRI to get a better idea of what we were dealing with. There was an 80% chance that the tumor would be malignant. The MRI results showed a solid mass that was probably a meningioma which is a persistent growing benign tumor. Why me? Why did I get the 20%?

After the surgery I lost most of the use of my left side, and I was in the hospital for three weeks going through physical therapy. God gave me so much strength that I not only recovered, but competed seven months later in the State power lifting competition and placed first, setting a record for my age and weight class in the bench press.

That's it!! This is why I'm here. I'm supposed to help people get in shape in case they ever have to fight a physical battle as I did. Being spiritually, mentally, and physically in shape increases the odds in your favor and makes recovery more possible. I got my personal trainers certification and decided I was going to volunteer down at the V.A. to help returning injured veterans build their strength back. I guess I should have asked first before setting that goal because union regulations would not allow volunteers in that capacity. I decided to volunteer at our church's fitness center with the same goal of helping people train.

In 2009, I went in for a check-up, and the pesky tumor was back. This time we decided on stereotactic radiation. A halo was bolted to my head (The only halo ever seen around my head, by the way), and low levels of radiation came in from all directions and met at the center of the tumor giving one massive dose.

I returned to volunteering at the fitness center, and then in 2013, you guessed it: the tumor was back again. This time it grew in such a way that it actually cut off the blood supply slowly over time through the sagittal vein that runs from the front of the head to the back. The body God created is amazing. While the tumor was growing, the body was finding new pathways. The surgeon cut the tumor out completely by snipping the vein on both sides. The surgery was on a Thursday, and the doctors couldn't believe the recovery this time. I was released on Saturday! A miracle. And back to work a week later. Why me? There has to be more. Why am I here??

Years later when our three children Katie, Aubrey, and Joey were grown and out of college, Karen and I decided to serve a few meals to the kids at St. Joe's Children's Home. We volunteered and took a couple of the kids out trick or treating one night. We were told bits of their backgrounds before we left; we were in shock. There is pure evil in this world, and these two boys had been severely abused. We were living life with blinders on. Both of us could not sleep for a few days following and went to church on Sunday as usual. We were praying for answers of what to do. Of all the Sundays in the 30 years we have been going to our church, when we walked in, it was ORPHAN SUNDAY. I could not look at Karen the whole service because I knew we would both lose it.

We signed up for foster parent classes and continued to volunteer at St. Joe's. We were approached by a staff member about a little girl we knew, and oh by the way, she had a sister. I asked some questions about what part of town they lived in at the time of their abuse and some other information. We decided to pray about becoming foster parents to these two little girls.

I began rereading a book called "God Winks." It's a book about how little, or sometimes how big things happen in people's lives, and it's like God winking at you. Around the same time at a Sunday church service, our minister Kyle Idleman introduced a pastor of a church that our church supports down in the west end of the city. That church was located on the exact same street where these little girls grew up. Chills started running up my spine, and I was feeling myself losing it a little. Could this be it? Could this be what we are supposed to do?

As Kyle was finishing his sermon, he said the words I will never forget, "Isn't it funny how sometimes things happen, and it's like God winking at you?" God wasn't winking at me; He was standing on a chair waving His arms, "Hey, you big dummy, what else do I have to do?"

We took in these two little girls for a time, but because of the severe trauma they had together, they were not able to remain together. Janie (not her name) needed way more special care than we could give her, and Courtney (not her name) returned to her previous foster mom. We are Godparents to Courtney, and she still comes over some weekends.

One day we got a call to foster another two little girls, one seven and the other almost two years old. It would only be for two weeks until they found a more permanent placement. I had always said "no diapers" in all our meetings, but then it would only be two weeks, right? We quickly realized we could not send these kids away at Christmas, and now here we are 10 months later, having fallen in love with them. We are Mommy and Poppy. There are still those days that make me want to bang my already dented head against the wall out of frustration, and then those days that make me melt. I now know why. Why me? I'm here to keep these kids safe and to give them a good home.

I'm not sure where this will lead. I know the direction we would like, but it's not up to us. Besides, I stopped planning a while back. God was having way too much fun watching me say never this or never that, and then putting me right in the middle of it. I know He belly laughs every time I change a poopy diaper.

That was one of those "I will never change another poopy diaper" things. Why me? This is why!!

Joe's verse: I can do everything through him who gives me strength. (Philippians 4:13)

My verse for Joe: Blessed is he who has regard for the weak; the LORD delivers him in times of trouble. (Psalm 41:1)

Annie Yoho, Personal Trainer, Yoho Fitness, Louisville, KY

Ann Carol is my sweet daughter and I don't see her the way she sees herself. She is fun and whimsical, bright, and resourceful. She has a strong faith, and without it, she could not have gotten through the tough year she had in 2014. She is an amazing inspiration to our family, friends, and complete strangers.

GOD PREPARED ME

He has made everything beautiful in His time . . .

I didn't feel beautiful when I looked in the mirror. After being diagnosed with breast cancer in February of 2014, I underwent a lumpectomy, and I was in the thick of my 20 weeks of chemo treatment. The lumpectomy left a large red scar on my right breast. I was completely bald and hairless, which meant no eyebrows and eyelashes either. You don't realize how much they frame your face until you don't have them. I looked blank. Even my eyelids were swollen, and what is worse, a blood vessel had popped in my left eye, so the white was now red. I had lost several pounds because I couldn't eat due to mouth sores, so my skin stretched over my bones. I resembled a creature from Pirates of the Caribbean. Before cancer ravaged my body, I had long silky hair -- and my eyes were my best feature. I was a personal trainer and had been a fitness fanatic most of my life. Now I was a sorry bag of bones.

The more I lost of my physical self, the more I was forced to face my vanity. With a bald head, bald face and scarred body -- I had a blank slate on the outside. I was forced to face my inner self, and it wasn't pretty either. Let's just say community service wasn't a high priority, and I didn't have much empathy for others. Mercy was on the bottom of my spiritual gift list.

In John 3:30, John the Baptist said, "He must become greater; I must become less." When we become less -- when we are blank - that's when He pours on some of His biggest blessings. And He did . . . just not in the way I expected.

Fast forward a few months. While I was undergoing radiation, through a series of God-inspired coincidences, I learned about LIVESTRONG -- a 12-week exercise and fitness program at the YMCA for anyone who has had cancer. It occurred to me that maybe I could volunteer? After all, what could be more perfect than a personal trainer-cancer-survivor all rolled into one? When I went to the Y to inquire about it, the director was so excited that she offered me a job on the spot. I have been with the LIVESTRONG program for two years now, and I know I have found my ministry.

God was preparing me for that moment since I taught group fitness in the 80's wearing leg warmers. He was equipping me with my personal trainer certification. He was refining me through my cancer. Cancer changed me in ways I could not have imagined. God did a work on me from the inside out. It opened my eyes to the pain and suffering of others and tenderized my heart. And God took that ugly disease and turned it into something beautiful.

And my hair? It grew back thick and curly. My scar has faded, but now when I see it in the mirror, I smile because I'm reminded that . . .

He makes ALL things beautiful in His time.

Annie's verse: Therefore, if anyone is in Christ, he is a new creation, the old has gone, the new has come! (2 Corinthians 5:17)

My verse for Ann Carol: Carry each other's burdens and in this way you will fulfill the law of Christ. (Galatians 6:2)

Nick Bonura, Photographer, Owner of Nick Bonura Photography, Louisville, KY

Nick is my youngest son, married to Nancy, and they have nine biological children. It is fun to visit in his home; there is always an additional child there, a friend's or neighbor's child who is getting in on the action. Nick is so easy-going and happy; he is always a delight to be around. He is a wonderful father.

IN A HEARTBEAT

On a recent tuck-in of my 4 year old daughter Janie, she looked up at me with her big blue eyes and asked me if she could listen to my heart. With a smile on my face, I gladly submitted. After giving her a turn, I got a turn listening to her heart too. When I hear it, I always look back into her eyes, hold her close, and tell her about how I cried the first time I heard it because I was so excited when I realized that she was alive. Although this may be one of those excuses for her to keep me in her room a little longer and therefore extend her bedtime, for me this has become one of those bed time rituals that I cherish.

You see, every time I hear her little heart beating, it reminds me of the first time I heard it at one of my wife's early pregnancy appointments. What a miracle, what an incredible miracle! My wife Nancy and I have 9 children and every time we have experienced hearing that heart beat and getting to see that tiny four chambered heart on an ultrasound, we cry and feel overwhelmed with God's blessing on us. I guess that is one of the reasons we have so many children. We love playing our small part in God's huge miracle of life.

When my Mom asked me to answer the question of where I have experienced God's majesty and bigness in my life, it wasn't hard to look right in front of me for the answer. God's awesome, creative, perfect majesty walks, talks, runs, jumps, laughs, learns, and lives right under the roof of my house. There is no other place in my life that I can marvel at God's bigness than in the lives of my children and in life itself.

It's interesting to contrast my little Janie's 4 year old heart to my grandfather Paw Paw's who died last year at the age of 96. His heart began beating almost 100 years ago and beat somewhere around 4 billion times. What made it start? Why did it keep beating after it started? It is unfathomable to think about all of the organs, tissues and systems that must work in perfect unity to keep us alive. With all of the technology that man has harnessed, all of the things that have been invented, all of the computers, micro-computers, cures for diseases, and biological milestones, the one thing that man can't do, and will never be able to do, is create life in any form from something that does not have life. The reason in my eyes is very clear: there is only one Creator, one incredible Designer of it all and that is God!

178

In April of 2016, a story broke that scientists from Northwestern University in Chicago, with the use of a powerful microscope, were able to see a literal flash of light at the moment of conception. Just think about that for a moment, at the very instant when the sperm penetrates the egg, God's finger reaches out and with fireworks, with what the scientists called an explosion of sparks, a human life is brought into the world. That is big, really big! For me, I see the bigness of God in what we are all guilty of taking for granted every day: we are alive!

Nick's verse: For we are God's workmanship, created in Christ Jesus to do good works, which God prepared in advance for us to do. (Ephesians 2:10)

My verse for Nick: My son, if your heart is wise, then my heart will be glad; my inmost being will rejoice when your lips speak what is right. (Proverbs 23:15-16)

Dorothy Mae Yokum, mother of six and lover of Jesus, Hammond, LA

This last entry is for my mother who died in 2004. Both she and my dad were very strong in their faith. Every night we knelt by the bed and prayed as a family, and my parents continued that practice until they died. Honesty and Integrity were their mottos. I write this story for my mother who experienced this amazing gift of God's love for her.

ALWAYS FAITHFUL

In 1999 my parents came to live in Louisville so that I could help Mother care for my dad who had Alzheimer's. My dad had always been very talkative and outgoing, always very strong and confident in his abilities. When he arrived in Louisville, little did I realize that he would be with us for a little over a year. His condition worsened and he could barely speak and he had no appetite for food. Mother was his primary caregiver, but she became very weak and finally she admitted that she could not care for him anymore.

Although it was extremely difficult to make the decision, Mother agreed that Dad needed to be placed in a skilled care facility. Mother visited him every day and remained with him until he retired in the evening. Each day found Dad losing another capacity or function. He could not feed himself, he could not speak or walk, and he was totally incontinent. He began to forget how to swallow, so how was he to get nourishment from food?

Mother realized after three months that her savings were depleting very quickly from the expenses of the skilled care facility. She worried about the situation, but she decided to simply trust God in the situation. (Of course, the family would be there to help, but Mother was always independent.)

My Dad lived only three months in the senior home when he finally passed away from all the complications of the Alzheimer's. The funeral arrangements were set in Louisiana where my parents had lived all their lives.

At the visitation, my mother was visited by her friend Bill from the Knights of Columbus, a Christian organization that my dad had belonged to when he lived in Louisiana. He gave my mother a check for $600, but she refused it and said to give half to her church and half to the Special Olympics (for people with intellectual disabilities). Those two areas were ones in which Mother and Dad volunteered in their senior years. Now, my mother certainly could have used that money for all the expenses from my dad's illness, but she always thought there was someone else who needed it more.

About six weeks after the funeral, my mother received a call from her friend Bill from the Knights of Columbus, and he told her that he had good news for her. He said, "Do you remember that money that you refused at the funeral? Well, we gave half to your church as you instructed us, and then we put the remaining $300 in a raffle that the Special Olympics was having. So we were still able to give that money to Special Olympics as you instructed. But we are happy to tell you that you won the raffle; you have won $10,000!!!" Mother could not believe what she was hearing. Her hands were trembling, and she was crying, happy tears.

Here is the God-thing: That $10,000 replaced the money that she had paid into the skilled care facility for my Dad, the exact amount to the dollar!! God is good, and He is merciful to his faithful ones.

Dorothy's verse: Psalm 23, I prayed it at her bedside when she was dying.

My verse for Mom: Well done, good and faithful servant! You have been faithful with a few things; I will put you in charge of many things. Come and share your master's happiness! (Matthew 25:21)

FINAL NOTE

I sn't it amazing to read all these astonishing perspectives of our great and loving God? Each person has had a divine encounter with the Almighty God.

A sweet friend Susan Douglas relates to me that she feels the awesomeness of God every time she studies the Bible—she finds another piece of the puzzle to understanding Him and His plan for her life. She is happiest when she is studying His Word, and she willingly shares her new knowledge with anyone with ears to hear. God has given us the Book in which He communicates with us; the more we study it, the better we know and love Him.

If you read each perspective of God in this book, you would quickly form a realization of His greatness. He is our Creator and our Refuge, a Healer and a Rescuer; He provides for our needs and gives us love and peace; He forgives and strengthens us. In His infinite goodness and mercy, He has provided a way to communicate with Him and a plan of salvation. God's purpose for this book may be to make the reader think more often about our powerful and all knowing God. He wants us to be more engaged with His presence. We have only a small insight into God's divine dimension, but even that glimpse is huge to us.

I took on the challenge of this book, but then Satan taunted me, causing doubt and loss of confidence. I felt incompetent and wondered who would read this book. I became fearful that no one would contribute to the stories in the book. I felt too old or too tired to do this project. I truly believe that God whispered in my husband Joe's ear and told Joe to encourage me to persevere in this book project. Just when I was feeling my lowest, Joe would lift me up and convince me that I could do it.

I am truly grateful to everyone who participated in this book. Their stories are certainly encouraging to those who have experienced similar situations. In many instances, the writers showed extreme bravery to bare such personal revelations.

I prayed and asked God to guide me through every step. God showed me those to ask to submit their stories. I take no credit; it was Holy Spirit led. To God be the glory!

I conclude with an appropriate quote from a famous physicist and mathematician Sir Isaac Newton who said of God, "He is eternal and infinite, omnipotent and omniscient; that is, his duration reaches from eternity to eternity; his presence from infinity to infinity." We cannot comprehend His extent. That is our Big God!

ABOUT THE AUTHOR

Carol Bonura is an active member of Southeast Christian Church where she was in the Care Ministry for 10 years visiting hospital patients to encourage and pray for them. Carol is an ardent student of the Bible and enjoys reading Christian novels and apologetics. She is a volunteer GED tutor at Necole's Place, a Christian life-skills and educational facility for women seeking pregnancy counseling.

Carol was born in New Orleans, Louisiana, and she presently resides in Louisville, Kentucky. She graduated with honors with a Bachelor of Arts degree in Art History from the University of Louisville. She was an art history researcher, and she was a docent at the Speed Art Museum for 15 years. She was Media Director of Bon Advertising Agency in Louisville for 16 years. She was director of the Metropolitan Opera Auditions for three years for the region that included Kentucky, Indiana, West Virginia, and Ohio.

She has been married to husband Joe for 53 years. They have three grown children and 15 grandchildren. Carol enjoys art, opera, reading, traveling, and Bible studies.

43833824R00113

Made in the USA
San Bernardino, CA
29 December 2016